Beyond Cloning

Beyond Cloning

Religion and
the Remaking
of Humanity

Edited by Ronald Cole-Turner

TRINITY PRESS INTERNATIONAL
Harrisburg, Pennsylvania

Trinity Press International, P.O. Box 1321, Harrisburg, PA 17105

Trinity Press International is a division of the Morehouse Group.

Cover design: Laurie Westhafer

Library of Congress Cataloging-in-Publication Data

Beyond cloning : religion and the remaking of humanity / edited by Ronald Cole-Turner.
 p. cm.
Includes bibliographical references and index.
ISBN 1-56338-317-9 (alk. paper)
 1 Genetic engineering—Religious aspects—Christianity. I. Cole-Turner, Ronald, 1948-

QH442 .B49 2001
261.5'5—dc21   00-047680

Printed in the United States of America

01 02 03 04 05 06   10 9 8 7 6 5 4 3 2 1

Contents

The Era of Biological Control

Ronald Cole-Turner

The technology of cloning that produced Dolly is a watershed development. But other new technologies, such as the ability to isolate and grow human stem cells, offer even greater and more immediate powers to control basic biological processes, especially as they apply to human health. The completion of the Human Genome Project now gives us unprecedented knowledge of the molecules that guide our developed. When we combine all these recent developments—cloning, stem cells, the genome, and genetic engineering—we have the basis for what Ian Wilmut calls the age of "biological control." How far will we go in using this power to control our own biology? How will we decide what limits should hold us back and what values should urge us on?

Dolly grabbed our attention in 1997 and shows no sign of letting go. More than all the world's ethicists and theologians combined, she has succeeded in getting us to focus our attention on the power of biological engineering to control our biology and to transform our nature.

At the same time, however, she has narrowed our gaze, for by our fixation on her, we have let ourselves become hyperfocused on one technique—reproductive cloning—as if it alone mattered. We have ignored other powerful technologies, and we have neglected the key question of how cloning fits within the pantheon of our new powers. Whatever one might think about the dangers of cloning, one real danger is that Dolly is a distraction.

Ian Wilmut, her maker, agrees. "Human cloning has grabbed people's imagination, but that is merely a diversion—and one we personally regret and find distasteful."[1] From what are we being diverted? From considering the ways in which cloning fits within a technological context, for according to Wilmut, "Our work completes the biotechnological trio: genetic engineering, genomics, and cloning."[2] We should spend less time on whether we should clone people and more on how cloning fits with other biological technologies that will soon give us the power to enter what Wilmut calls the "age of biological control." As important as it may be to ask about human reproductive cloning, we dare not limit our moral gaze to this one application or restrict the scope of our moral view to this one technique. Our deliberation about cloning is too often confined to asking only the simplest questions, such as how soon it can be done and when it will be safe. We have not asked where cloning is taking us. Cloning is part of a package, not a stand-alone technology, and if we are to understand it at all, we must view it within its full technological context. What is the full scope of this power that is soon to be in our hands, and what on earth are we to do with it? *That* is the key question.

Cloning—sometimes called nuclear transfer, sometimes nuclear replacement—involves the transfer of the DNA nucleus from a cell to an egg from which the nucleus has been removed. Ian Wilmut and Keith Campbell made history when they did this in sheep, starting with a cell from an adult ewe, transferring its nucleus to an egg from another ewe, and implanting it in yet another ewe, who gave birth to Dolly. For many people, the word *cloning* means creating a new sheep, maybe a new human being. That definition is too narrow for geneticists, who use the word *cloning* to mean copying or replicating any DNA, from short stretches to the entire nucleus or genome. Little wonder, then, that geneticists were alarmed at some legislative attempts to ban cloning as understood by the popular definition. Some of these bills had the effect of banning all replication of DNA or cloning by the geneticists' definition, and that would have shut down their work entirely. Nevertheless, despite the technical use of the word by geneticists, our use here lies closer to the popular definition, involving the transfer of the whole nucleus of DNA from one cell to anoth-

---

1. Ian Wilmut in Ian Wilmut, Keith Campbell, and Colin Tudge, *The Second Creation: Dolly and the Age of Biological Control* (New York: Farrar, Straus and Giroux, 2000), p. 11.

2. Ibid.

er, usually to an egg, in order to begin an embryo. But where the public most often thinks of that embryo being implanted and resulting in a child, we include other purposes besides reproduction.

What cloning offers is the power to reverse cell differentiation, a natural process whereby the cells of the developing body become different from each other, even though they share the same genes, so that one is a brain cell whereas another is a muscle cell or a blood cell. Until Dolly, scientists believed that cell differentiation was generally irreversible in mammals. "Differentiation in general merely requires the shutting down of genes, and what is shut down, so it now seems, can be switched on again."[3] This power to move an entire nucleus so that it can become an embryo, to dedifferentiate its nuclear DNA, is a technology of sweeping implications.

One way to understand the power of cloning is to think about its potentially important relationship to human germ line modification. As a project, germ line modification is far more audacious than cloning, for whereas cloning might create a new individual with nuclear DNA taken from another, germ line modification intentionally *alters* the DNA that an individual inherits and transmits to future generations. Cloning replicates genes that have existed, but germ line modification creates something new and possibly enhanced. Such germ line modification has been achieved in animals, but with low efficiency and safety. This work is done in farm animals, for instance, in order to introduce human genes into sheep so that the sheep will produce valuable human proteins for therapies. Indeed, the reason why Wilmut and Campbell produced Dolly in the first place was to increase the efficiency of germ line modification.

Human germ line modification has not yet been attempted, but it is being discussed seriously and it has vocal advocates.[4] One of

3. Ian Wilmut and Keith Campbell, "The New Biotechnology," in Ian Wilmut, Keith Campbell, and Colin Tudge, *The Second Creation*, p. 264.

4. For a critical discussion, see Mark S. Frankel and Audrey R. Chapman, editors, *Human Inheritable Genetic Modification: Assessing Scientific, Ethical, Religious, and Policy Issues* (Washington, D.C.: American Association for the Advancement of Science, 2000). For advocates of human germ line modification, see Gregory Stock and John Campbell, editors, *Engineering the Human Germ Line: An Exploration of the Science and Ethics of Altering the Genes We Pass to Our Children* (New York: Oxford University Press, 2000).

the strongest arguments against it is the low reliability of all current gene modification techniques. Before one would consider starting a genetically altered human embryo down the pathway of development to a live baby, one would have to be quite sure that the genetic alteration has been done right. Cloning may make it possible to have this confidence by introducing a kind of verification process, and so it is altogether likely that if we cross the threshold to germ line modification, it will be because cloning has paved the way, technically speaking. Our current level of success with germ line modification techniques in animals is too low to be acceptable for human use, "but with cloning, the entire equation changes. Now, multiple cells grown from a single embryo could be subjected to genetic engineering" and the successfully altered embryos might then be implanted.[5]

Exactly what role could cloning or nuclear DNA transfer play in opening the way to germ line modification? A detailed explanation of the relationship between cloning and germ line modification is offered by Mario Capecchi, who describes one likely approach:

> In vitro fertilization using sperm and eggs donated by each set of parents would be used to generate one-cell embryos. . . . In culture, the embryo would be permitted to progress to the four-cell stage. The embryo would then be separated into four cells; three of these cells would be frozen for later use. These are procedures routinely carried out in IVF clinics. Each of these four cells, frozen or unfrozen, would have an identical set of genes and would be capable of generating a normal child. The fourth cell would be allowed to divide in culture until a million cells were generated, taking approximately twenty cell divisions to achieve this number. Different embryonic cell types would be present within this cell population, but this diversity should not affect the procedure. One million cells is an ample population size to permit the use of technologies, such as gene targeting, to introduce the desired genetic alteration into a subset of these cells. The subset of cells containing the desired genetic alteration would be isolated from the remaining cell population and carefully characterized to ensure that the genet-

---

5. Lee M. Silver, *Remaking Eden: How Genetic Engineering and Cloning Will Transform the American Family* (New York: Avon Books, 1997), p. 152.

ic modification was accurate. At this point, the nucleus of one of the mother's oocytes would be removed and replaced with the nucleus from the expanded pool of cells containing the prescribed genetic modification. In this cytoplasmic environment, the modified nucleus would receive instructions to commence making an embryo. The cells would be allowed to divide in culture once or twice, and then the embryo would be surgically transferred to the mother's womb to allow pregnancy to continue. A child produced in this way would contain the genetic modification, introduced in cell culture, in all of his or her cells, including the germ cells.[6]

If so, it becomes even clearer that all discussions about cloning that ignore human germ line modification suffer from a kind of moral tunnel vision grounded in a misunderstanding of biotechnology. And yet nearly all the ethics debates about cloning have overlooked this relationship, often ignoring the question of human germ line modification altogether.

Dolly may also be diverting our attention from advances in stem cell technology and how cloning may be involved here, too. In late 1998, success in isolating human stems cells was reported.[7] These cells appear to have the capacity to differentiate into any kind of human cell. During normal development, cells differentiate along precisely defined pathways so that some cells become neurons and others, for example, make up the pancreas or muscles. Stem cells are at the beginning of that process of differentiation and have the capacity to follow any of these pathways to become any kind of cell. Researchers were able to isolate these cells

6. Mario R. Capecchi, "Human Germ Line Gene Therapy: How and Why," Stock and Campbell, *Engineering the Human Germline, An Exploration of the Science and Ethics of Altering the Genes We Pass to our Children* (New York: Oxford University Press, 2000), p. 35.

7. James A. Thomson, Joseph Itskovitz-Eldor, Sander S. Shapiro, Michelle A. Waknitz, Jennifer J. Swiergiel, Vivienne S. Marshall, and Jeffrey M. Jones. "Embryonic Stem Cell Lines Derived from Human Blastocysts," *Science,* 282 (1998): 1145-1147; and M.J. Shamblott, J. Axelman, S. Wang, E.M. Bugg, J.W. Littlefield, P.J. Donovan, P.D. Blumenthal, G.R. Huggins, J.D. Gearhart, "Derivation of Pluripotent Stem Cells from Cultured Human Primordial Germ Cells," *Proceedings of the National Academy of Science of the United States of America,* 95 (1998): 13726-31.

and to keep them in a state of perpetual non-differentiation. Their hope is that they can coax these cells along specific pathways in order to produce large numbers of cells for implantation in specific organs or tissues in human beings. For instance, those suffering from brain degeneration would receive cells that are progressing along the pathway to becoming neurons. Implanted, the new cells will multiply and replace the old cells, perhaps taking up the function that the damaged cells can no longer perform.

How does cloning fit in? Perhaps in several ways, but one of the more immediate is that cloning may help solve the problem of tissue rejection. When cells are implanted, the body's natural immune response is to kill them. This response can be suppressed with drugs, but suppressing the immune system is hardly ideal. If the patient's own nuclear DNA could be put into the stem cells, perhaps by using some form of the Dolly nuclear transfer technique to create an embryo from which stem cells were derived, just for each patient, then it might be possible to overcome the problem of immune response.

This merging of stem cell and cloning technology would open the way for widespread use of stem cells, which hold great promise for treating many diseases and injuries, from burns and spinal cord injuries to organ failure and brain degeneration. So great is this promise, in fact, that we can begin to see that stem cell technology may usher in a day when human beings routinely have their tissues and organs not exactly replaced but rejuvenated. It is hard to argue against the use of stem cells to treat injuries or the effects of degenerative diseases, although many are of course deeply troubled by the way in which stem cells are derived, either from fetal tissue or by destroying an embryo. This problem is all the worse if we imagine a form of future medicine that creates an embryo by cloning from each patient in order to avoid immune rejection. It is possible that research will find a way around this problem, but until it does, not everyone will accept stem cell medicine.

Nevertheless, stem cells may give us the ability to rejuvenate tissues and organs. We may learn to forestall the aging process itself. Implanted stem cells may bring youthfulness to aging organs and, by extension, to aging bodies. In fact, it may be possible to alter these cells so that they are enhanced over the cells with which the patient began life in the first place. For instance, it may be possible to alter cells prior to implantation so that they resist disease, improve brain function, and do not age. I expect that this use of cloning—to create stem cells for tissue regeneration and enhancement—will be the most significant and widely used application of cloning. Combined with other technologies, modified stem cell techniques will probably extend the human life span, perhaps significantly. This will mean not just that individuals will live longer because they will not die of certain diseases. It means we will age more slowly and may live to 150 years, 200, or longer.

But surely, cloning's most ardent opponents will say that now we are getting off the subject. The question we must face today is not the doubling of our lifespans but the immediate question posed by Dolly, the question of producing a baby as Dolly was produced. It is not Dolly who is diverting us but the confusing expansion of her significance to include all these other technologies and their futuristic applications. Shifting our focus from cloning to such things as germ line modification and stem cell technology is just another way to take our attention away from our most pressing moral problem in biotechnology, namely, how to ban reproductive cloning forever. Here is the place to draw the bright line, to say no if it is still possible to say no, and to insist that the pathway of biotechnological development steer a wide course around human reproductive cloning. Wilmut's complaints of "diversion" are themselves a diversion. Reproductive cloning *is* the issue, and efforts to focus on so-called broader questions are a ploy, really designed to get us to focus on small steps, which, taken one at a time, will arouse little opposition, but which when completed will bring us to a world in which reproductive cloning is a fait accompli.

It is falsely reassuring, cloning's opponents will continue, to hear that Dolly's makers do not want to make babies. Granted, Wilmut claims "that the prospect of human cloning causes us grave misgivings. It is physically too risky, it could have untoward effects on the psychology of the cloned child, and in the end we see no medical justification for it."[8] But has he not set us on a pathway

8. Wilmut, *The Second Creation,* p. 5.

of animal cloning and nonreproductive human applications that can only give us what he claims to dislike? Has he not lit the fuse under the rocket so that even he is unable to cancel the launch?

Consider, for instance, the position of the government in the United Kingdom regarding the use of cloning (or "cell nuclear replacement") to produce embryos for research. Noting the promise of great medical benefits in treating degenerative diseases, the government report recommends that "research using embryos (whether created by in vitro fertilization or cell nuclear replacement) to increase understanding about human disease and disorders and their cell-based treatments should be permitted."[9] Just before reaching this conclusion, however, the report acknowledges that "concerns have also been expressed that allowing research on embryos created by cell nuclear replacement would be a first step on a 'slippery slope' towards human reproductive cloning. The Expert Group concluded that an inadvertent slide into reproductive cloning was not a realistic prospect because of the stringent controls operated in the UK by the Human Fertilisation and Embryology Authority [which] will not license the implantation of embryos created by nuclear replacement."[10]

Cloning's ardent opponents, and any who sympathize with persons of strong principle when they are backed into a moral quandary, will find this policy deeply disturbing. What is its most likely result? That by cloning, embryos will be created for research purposes. And the simple existence of these cloned embryos changes the morally relevant facts of the situation by creating a new reality to which all must respond. How are we to respond to the existence of these cloned embryos? What are they, and what do we owe them? If they are *persons*, must they not be implanted? In other words, if nonreproductive cloning proceeds, as it soon will, are we not likely to have backed ourselves into a peculiar situation in which cloning's strongest opponents will find that their own moral logic forces them to support the reproductive conclusion to

9. The Chief Medical Officer's Expert Group, Department of Health, The United Kingdom, *Stem Cell Research: Medical Progress with Responsibility* (London, June 2000), 10.

10. Ibid.

the act of cloning? Those who believe these embryos are persons and entitled to the same respect and protection accorded any other human being will be forced by their convictions to *demand* that cloned embryos not be destroyed but made available to those who would implant them and bring them alive into the world. This is no slippery slope. It is a moral necessity, at least for those who accept the premise concerning embryos. And yet public policy proceeds as if we can disconnect the argument about reproductive cloning from the argument about nonreproductive cloning and that we may permit the one while pretending to prohibit the other.

In the United States, public policy on these matters is less clear and consistent than elsewhere. The position of the United States, advanced by the National Institutes of Health but by no means widely accepted or established beyond the possibility of congressional review, is that all things are permitted, but almost nothing is funded. Work with stem cells derived from embryos is eligible for funds, at least for now, but no funds may be spent directly on embryo research or on the derivation of stem cells from embryos or fetuses, much less on the creation of embryos by cloning. Banning the use of federal funds is a weak ban, however. Private funds may be used legally to create cloned embryos and indeed to implant them or to modify them using genetic engineering.

It is little wonder that cloning evokes such sharply negative reactions, all the more intense because we seem to have no way to *hear* them or allow their arguments to count in the formation of policy, at least as long as they remain in a political minority. I am not among "cloning's most ardent critics," but I do believe we benefit from their arguments, not merely to challenge our thinking, but to change its conclusions where it counts most immediately: in the shaping of public policy that reflects the best wisdom a pluralistic society can educe.

Some have opposed cloning by declaring that it is repugnant and that we should respond with revulsion. Cloning, according to Leon Kass, belongs in the same category as incest, sex with animals, mutilating a corpse, eating human flesh, rape, and murder.[11]

---

11. Leon Kass, "The Wisdom of Repugnance," in Leon Kass and James Q. Wilson, *The Ethics of Human Cloning* (Washington, D.C.: American Enterprise Institute Press, 1998), 18-19.

But not everyone finds cloning repugnant. Some find it fascinating, even irresistible. They may be wrong about that, but so may Kass. What we need to recognize is that human reproductive cloning at once repulses and fascinates us, and those who oppose it most would do well not only to show us why its fascinations are of the same kind as the forbidden fruit, but also to recognize that cloning may be attractive *because* it is wrong.

For Christians this is all familiar ground, for there is nothing new about being warned of the attractions of evil and the seductiveness of temptation. Is cloning attractive for the wrong reasons? Is it pure evil masquerading as the "Killer App," or is it a limited good that comes with a long list of possibly dangerous side effects, which we can avoid if we are careful? Perhaps the general public has understood something about cloning that the experts have ignored, namely, that cloning appeals to us because we desire power over nature, over life, over our own bodies. We fear age, degeneration, and loss of mental powers more than death itself. Here is a technology that turns back biological time, that promises to rejuvenate cells and organs and, most of all, brains. Is this evil masquerading as good? Is it access to the tree of life via the tree of knowledge, and are we too blind to see the evil? Is cloning quite literally a wolf in sheep's clothing?

Even to begin to answer these questions, we have to see that cloning comes to us in a technological context that itself is embedded within a cultural context. It is as if cloning comes to us nested in a matrix of technologies, which in turn is nested in a context of culture. No new technology, after all, simply emerges on its own, nor do tools just fall from the sky. Technology as a whole, including the wide range of biotechniques of which cloning is but one part, is itself embedded within a cultural context of values, patterns, taboos, and traditional mores and practices, all of which flow together to evoke a technology, to call it forth in its design and its perceived necessity, until it is invented. Culture creates and defines "problems," or at the very least prioritizes problems such as diseases that technology then "solves" or upon which medicine wages "war." Technology's cultural context sets values on techniques and brings consumers together with suppliers through economic institutions and brokerages, a means of exchange by which the owners and providers of technology sell access to their powers to consumers for private ends.

Nowhere is this technology marketplace more in evidence than in reproductive medicine as it is currently practiced in the United States. Consumers, usually infertile couples, contract with technology providers for a range of services that fit their needs and desires. Questions of value become mere questions of price, constrained by the efficiency of the "product" and what price the market will bear. It has even been suggested that this model of a laissez-faire technology flea market should serve as the prototype for the social and economic system that manages the development of reproductive cloning and human germ line modification. At a symposium on germ line modification, Lee M. Silver offered this advice: "I don't see why you need extra regulations for germ line engineering. The IVF-clinic model in America seems to be working quite well for the most part. You can extend this [to germ line modification]."[12]

You do not need to be opposed to germ line modification to reject the suggestion that this cultural system, the unregulated and largely unaccountable in vitro clinic, should be the preferred way in which these technologies will be developed and regulated. In such a system, we would expect that individual consumers will contract with unregulated providers for these emerging technologies—not yet available but soon to come—to try to attain children with altered genes thought to match parents' hopes. The hopes of parents may be lofty and well intended, but they will of course reflect the cultural context that evokes these emerging technologies in the first place. What can we say about this context? It is characterized by individualism, competitiveness, parental anxieties, freedom from regulation or oversight, and privatization of decisions. In such a context, the anxieties of parents will be readily exploited when they hear what other parents, more committed to their children, are doing to improve their offspring's inheritance.

Furthermore, the cultural context that creates these technologies includes the widely held belief that we *are* our genes, and that if we can just alter our children's genes and improve them, we will have better children or at least children who better match our

---

12. Lee M. Silver, comment made in a panel discussion at the conference "Engineering the Human Germ line," Los Angeles, March 1998, in Stock and Campbell, *Engineering the Human Germ line*, p. 89.

desires. This belief, "genetic determinism," coupled with all the competitive anxieties of parenthood in an unregulated free market of gene modification technologies in the IVF clinic model, should be enough to make germ line technology's *advocates* cringe.

If this convergence of technology and culture correctly describes the future, then the best we can hope for is that we will have a lot of future parents who feel swindled, having paid for modifications that did not bring the hoped-for results. What will parents want? Healthier, taller, smarter, thinner, more gregarious, children who are athletic, attractive, and light-skinned. Now it may become possible someday to alter genes associated with these traits, but whether changing these genes will produce any observable outcome, desired or not, remains to be seen. Mistakes will be made, and children will be born with unforeseen problems. The path to the "age of biological control" is strewn with many technical difficulties. Most parents will be disappointed, and when that happens, we will fear for their children.

But the even greater danger is that these technologies may succeed, at least in part, and that they may actually offer what people are looking for in the way of the power to define their offspring. If so, then the small-scale, private decisions of thousands, perhaps millions of parents, taken in the aggregate, *become* the collective decision of humanity. In Silver's model, there is no open consensus building, no public debate, no moment in which we human beings acknowledge that we stand together at a fateful threshold of a radically different future and decide together to take the step or to close the door. There is only the individual or at best a couple, making micro decisions that lead, one by one, across a threshold that affects every human being on the planet. If we clone, if we engage in germ line modification, it will be a human act that forever changes humanity.

A strategy of convenience for some seems to be to keep the decisions small, too small for public review, and to keep them centered in the technologically permissive environment of countries like the United States. According to Daniel Koshland Jr., former editor of the journal *Science*, "It seems to me the United States will be in the forefront of this research. We're more likely to carry it out successfully than almost any nation in the world. To try and get all the nations of Europe to agree with us, let alone all Africa and Asia, will significantly hinder us. If we go ahead and set a successful example, most people will want to follow that example."[13] It is entirely possible that they, our planetary co-inhabitants, will not want to follow and that they will deeply resent our having excluded them from asking whether we should take the step.

It is not for any one person, group of people, religious tradition, or nation to decide the question. How then do we create the public structures of debate? How does *humanity* reach a decision on cloning, germ line modification, or the use of stems cells or other technologies?

In particular, how do we bring the insight of one religious tradition, Christianity, to bear upon the public deliberation? This is the question posed to the authors of the chapters that follow. We do not agree on the answer, but we agree that in the balance hangs the future.

---

13. Daniel Koshland Jr., comment made in a panel discussion at the conference "Engineering the Human Germ line," Los Angeles, March 1998, in Stock and Campbell, *Engineering the Human Germ line*, p. 87.

A Christian Physician at the Crossroads of New Genetic Technologies and the Needs of Patients

Kenneth W. Culver, M.D.

*Working with W. French Anderson and Michael Blaese,
Kenneth Culver made history in 1990 when as a physician he
administered the first human gene therapy trials. Since then, he
has remained at the forefront of developments that apply the
powers of genetic engineering to human health, believing that
this work is his way to live out his faith and his calling to follow
Jesus Christ in today's high-tech world. Culver provides us with
a road map of these developments and an assessment of their
potential value for human health.*

As a young physician in training, I was assigned to the neonatal
intensive care unit (NICU). Each day we struggled with how to
apply new technologies in the treatment of life-threatening situations. We used every new machine, medication, and novel technique to save the lives of premature babies. During this intense and
challenging experience, I constantly tried to understand why children were born premature or with severe congenital abnormalities. But the most haunting question I faced was why we did not
have curative therapies to help these fragile human lives.

One day a mother of a child dying from bone marrow failure
due to an underlying genetic disorder asked, "How can you keep a
positive attitude while doing this difficult work?" I told her that I
was entrusting to God that which I did not understand, even to the
point of entrusting God with the outcome of our limited attempts

to heal these children. Believing that our loving God was in control was indeed the only way I could successfully cope with the struggles and heartache in caring for these desperately ill children.

Over the years of caring for many children with life-threatening genetic disorders, I found myself increasingly frustrated with the inability of traditional treatments to cure my patients. Since new treatments were coming along regularly, it seemed to me that God was revealing to researchers the world over the new insights that someday would lead to the curative therapies we all desired. So I became a researcher for just that reason: so that I could join the effort to understand how to apply new knowledge that might help the children in my care. For my generation, the overwhelming new information has been in genetics. This personal desire to unlock the secrets of using genes to treat human disease ultimately led to a passion for working toward and implementing the first approved gene therapy experiment in 1990.[1,2]

As a follower of Jesus Christ, I found that I was guided and inspired by the stories of his healing ministry in the New Testament. For instance, Matthew 14:14 states, "When Jesus landed and saw a large crowd, he had compassion on them and healed their sick." The apostles also had compassion for the sick, healing many during their ministries. I, too, feel that same calling as a physician-scientist, as if my work in the NICU and in the genetics lab were my personal form of discipleship.

Not just Christians but our society at large embraces the right of all people to have the opportunity to seek healing. Compassion for the sick is a powerful motivator for action. Whether persons who are sick alter their diet, take vitamins, swallow a pill, or are treated with a new gene, the goal is the same: the healing of the sick because of compassion for them.

---

1. R.M. Blaese, K.W. Culver, and W.F. Anderson, "The ADA Human Gene Therapy Clinical Protocol," *Human Gene Therapy*, 1 (1990): 331-362.

2. R.M. Blaese, K.W. Culver, A.D. Miller, C.S. Carter, T. Fleisher, M. Clerici, G. Shearer, L.Chang, Y. Chiang, P. Tolstoshev, J.J. Greenblatt, S.A. Rosenberg, H. Klein, M.Berger, C.A. Mullen, W.J. Ramsey, L. Muul, R.A. Morgan, and W.F. Anderson, "T Lymphocyte-Directed Gene Therapy for ADA- SCID: Initial Trial Results after 4 Years," *Science*, 270 (1995): 475-480.

Treatment	Current Examples or Potential Applications
Small-molecule drugs and immunizations	*Classical drugs like Tylenol, codeine, and insulin*
Solid-organ transplantation	*Liver and kidney, for example*
Bone marrow transplantation	*For the treatment of bone marrow failure and cancer*
Monoclonal antibodies	*Herceptin for the treatment of breast cancer*
Somatic cell gene therapy (gene transfer)	*Inherited disorders, cancer, infectious diseases, and cardiovascular diseases*
Somatic cell gene repair	*Inherited disorders, cancer, infectious diseases, and cardiovascular diseases*
Stem cell transplantation	*Inherited disorders*
Germ line genetic modification	*Inherited disorders*
Nuclear transfer and cloning	*Nuclear transfer for inherited disorders*

New medical technologies, especially those based on genetics, are not without their problems. Any new treatment carries risks. Some people think that applying genetics to human health simply goes too far, that it amounts to "playing God." I disagree, of course, and I continue to pursue genetics research to benefit human health. But it is important that the public understands where this research is going so that people can help define the directions and the limits of these new techniques. In this chapter, therefore, I plan to review the burgeoning new genetic technologies in development in contrast to traditional therapies. These new therapeutics have the potential dramatically to improve health care in the future and in some cases raise new ethical concerns that deserve discussion. The accompanying table delineates a range of available technologies and includes some that will soon move to the clinic for experimentation. The list runs the gamut of traditional, well-characterized therapies to highly experimental treatments that are being considered for the distant future. After I discuss each of the techniques, I will offer a few personal concluding remarks.

SMALL-MOLECULE DRUGS AND IMMUNIZATIONS

The most common therapies available for the treatment and prevention of human disease are small-molecule drugs and immunizations. Small-molecule drugs usually consist of chemicals that are formulated into tablets, capsules, and inhalers. While many small-molecule drugs have shown clear benefits to patients, in most cases, these treatments are symptomatic and fail to treat the underlying basis of the disorder (e.g., antihistamines for allergies). In addition, they are applied empirically without the knowledge of who will respond to a particular drug better or worse than another individual.

Fortunately, this type of drug prescribing will improve in the near future. As a consequence of advances in genetics, we are now beginning to understand how subtle changes in genes can lead to differential responses to commonly used drugs. For example, we know that some individuals will get very good pain relief from codeine while others will not. In many cases, this discrepancy can be explained by subtle changes in a single chemical base component of DNA, called a polymorphism. In other words, a subtle change in one chemical base in a drug-metabolizing gene can lead to an alteration in drug metabolism by the patient.

These polymorphisms can lead to markedly slowed or very fast metabolism of drugs. Individuals who have genetically slowed metabolism of drugs can experience major differences in therapeutic benefit. If the drug metabolism gene is responsible for inactivation of the drug, then slowed inactivation means the drug may accumulate to very high levels and lead to undesired adverse consequences. On the other hand, if the role of the drug metabolism gene is to activate the drug, then slowed or absent activation will limit efficacy. One clear example of this difference between patients occurs with codeine, a common pain reliever.[3] The CYP2D6 drug-metabolizing

3. S.V. Otton, M. Schadel, S.W. Cheung, H.L. Kaplan, U.E. Busto, and E.M. Sellers, "CYP2D6 Phenotype Determines the Metabolic Conversion of Hydrocodone to Hydromorphone," *Clinical Pharmacology and Therapeutics*, 54 (1993): 463-472.

gene metabolizes codeine and turns it into morphine. It is not the codeine but its metabolism to morphine that is responsible for the pain relief. If the CYP2D6 gene is altered in some way so that the conversion to morphine is absent or limited, the patient will get the adverse effects associated with codeine but not have any of the anticipated analgesic effect.

While these genetic tools will help us decide which drug is the best for a particular patient, this approach to human disease in most cases is not leading to a cure. Whole new therapies are required as part of our therapeutic armament adequately to address the variety of health problems that exist in our population. The future here for small-molecule drugs is bright in part because we are now beginning to understand not only the genetics behind healthy responses and adverse reactions to drugs but also the molecular mechanisms of action. For years, the mechanism of action of drugs like aspirin, for instance, was not definitely known. As a result, drug development was hit or miss, trial and error. Advances in genetics will help us unravel the exact pathways by which drugs do their work. This new, detailed understanding will help us develop drugs that specifically target genetic pathways that need modification without altering other processes that may lead to adverse consequences.

This is how new antihistamine drugs have been developed to eliminate the sedation associated with older antihistamines. However, new and powerful levels of understanding of the genetic processes underlying disease states will take us well beyond the making of better antihistamines or other commonly used medications. For instance, it may be possible one day to prevent the development of malformed hearts with small-molecule drugs. This may be done by first identifying a family at risk and then administering the proper drug at the time of heart formation in utero to overcome the genetic problem, thereby preventing the malformation. When I was a pediatric resident, we could only dream of such a therapy. As more and more genes involved in human maladies are identified, the variety of creative new uses for small-molecule drugs will significantly increase.

From an ethical perspective, the use of small-molecule drugs is widely accepted in our society. It is also well understood that there are many circumstances in which small-molecule drugs are inadequate, justifying more heroic treatments like organ transplantation and gene therapy. However, as the understanding of genetics grows, the number of conditions that will be treatable with small-molecule drugs will expand, limiting the need for these heroic therapies. Immunizations will also move forward in the future, thanks in part to genetics. Traditional vaccines have been here for more than two hundred years, and their widespread use has had a profound effect all over the world for decades. Immunizations were initially designed to prevent viral and bacterial infections, but they are now being developed as a means to instruct the immune system specifically to target and destroy proteins, antibodies, cells, chemicals, and drugs.

For example, immunizations are being developed to inactivate cocaine to treat drug abuse, to protect people from the development of multiple sclerosis, and to inactivate a variety of new infectious agents like HIV.[4] Immunizations have the potential for disease prevention, which is always better than trying to eliminate a disease process after it has begun. Therefore, it is not surprising that the growth in the genetic understanding of human disease and the immune system will lead to new ways to solve health problems in humans with genetic immunizations.

In the future, immunizations will most likely involve the injection of genes to induce the desired immune responses. Currently, when a live, attenuated virus is injected into the human body, like many current immunizations, it is the expression of the virus genes in the infected cells that leads to a protective immune response. Instead of risking adverse reactions with live viruses, scientists can remove the relevant viral genes and inject them, where they are expressed inducing a protective immune response. This is much safer, far less expensive, and allows for the simultaneous protection against multiple organisms at the same time. Thanks to genetic research, the immunizations of the future will be safer and more effective, and will be given with one injection by mixing genes from multiple infectious agents. In addition, they will not be limited to the prevention of infectious disease, but will be used for the prevention of many types

---

4. M.R. Carrera, J.A. Ashley, L.H. Parsons, P. Wirsching, G.F. Koob, and K.D. Janda, "Suppression of Psychoactive Effects of Cocaine by Active Immunization," *Nature,* 378 (1995): 727-730.

of acquired diseases where the genetic components are understood, such as cancer and autoimmune diseases.

From an ethical point of view, immunizations have been well accepted in our society. In fact, we require immunizations for children in developed countries, and we applaud efforts to make them available worldwide. So I anticipate that the advances in this area that come about because of genetics will be broadly welcomed.

SOLID-ORGAN TRANSPLANTATION

It should have been no surprise that artificial heart transplants were performed in humans because of the desperate need of those with failed hearts. The high-profile transplant of the fully mechanical Jarvik-7 artificial heart into Barney Clark in 1982, however, was disappointing. Human heart transplants have been performed since 1967, but the results have not been perfect, and so the mechanical heart was developed. Other efforts to compensate for or replace the failing human heart have also included the transplant of baboon and chimpanzee hearts into humans. One problem, of course, is that the human body's immune system rejects implanted organs. However, as a result of the discovery of potent antirejection medications, tens of thousands of solid-organ transplants have occurred around the world in recent years. This includes not only heart transplants but also liver, lung, intestinal, pancreatic, kidney, cornea, skin, and hand transplants.

Why have these transplants been so widely adopted as part of accepted medical practice? In part, because small-molecule therapy has been unable to heal the underlying disease processes and there is no other therapeutic choice. For instance, current small-molecule drugs are highly effective in controlling hypertension but not in stopping the progression of arteriosclerosis that leads to progressive narrowing of the arteries and loss of organ function. For people who over many years have developed irreversible organ damage due either to an underlying genetic condition, environmental causes, or lifestyle choices, the only hope is the transfer of a new, healthy organ.

Because of the shortage of organs, many people die while waiting for an organ transplant. There is a significant global effort underway to develop organs for transplantation from pigs.[5] Using genetic modification techniques, components of pig cells that lead to rejection by the new human host are being eliminated. Researchers hope that success in these experiments will make organs available for many who are on the waiting lists. But because there may be a number of unknown risks associated with pig organ transplantation, there is an extensive effort to understand the implications of pig-to-human transplants before widespread use begins. A careful monitoring program is being developed so that any unexpected problems may be quickly identified and traced back to the source to improve the safety of future applications.

The need for transplanted organs will likely be reduced in the future due to the use of improved small-molecule drugs, immunizations, gene therapy, and/or stem cell transplants. Since the hepatitis virus is one of the common reasons for liver failure leading to the need for a liver transplant, new immunizations may reduce the need for transplantable livers. Later I will discuss gene therapy and stem cell transplants. These strategies may also have the potential for treating the fundamental basis of the disease, leading to full correction of the disease and its manifestations. Therefore, the use of pig organs will likely be an interim solution for those whose life cannot be sustained in any other way.

From an ethical point of view, the transfer of solid-organs has been widely accepted because it is seen as a last resort for people who have no other alternative. This is a common theme that runs through the development of many of the technologies discussed in this chapter. As long as our society embraces the perspective that each person should be permitted the opportunity to recover from the devastations of disease, solid-organ transplantation will proceed. From a scientific point of view, solid-organ transplantation has greatly improved over the past several decades. While problems with organ rejection remain, the prognosis for people with terminal diseases, potentially treatable by solid-organ transplantation, has markedly

---

5. K. Paradis, G. Langford, Z. Long, W. Heneine, P. Sandstrom, W.M. Switzer, L.E. Chapman, C. Lockey, D. Onions, and E. Otto, "Search for Cross-Species Transmission of Porcine Endogenous Retrovirus in Patients Treated with Living Pig Tissue," *Science,* 285 (1999): 1236-1241.

improved. The primary influences that will decrease the pressure for solid-organ transplantation are a cultural shift to healthier lifestyle choices (e.g., elimination of tobacco smoking), improved small-molecule drugs, new immunizations, and the advent of genetic therapies. These technologies have the possibility of preventing disease, slowing the progression of organ failure, and/or healing the organ.

BONE MARROW TRANSPLANTATION

Bone marrow transplantation is another therapy that has been developed out of necessity because of the failure of traditional small-molecule therapeutics. Unlike solid-organ transplantation, the majority of bone marrow transplants are performed as the treatment for cancer. One of the primary consequences of chemotherapy is the destruction of bone marrow cells. This occurs because the chemotherapy is not exclusively targeted to the tumor cell, but rather targets all cells that are actively proliferating, like bone marrow, skin, and intestinal tract cells. Cancer cells by definition are cells that are continually growing without proper regulatory control. If unstopped, the cancerous cells eventually lead to widespread tissue destruction. In order to save patients from the extreme toxicities associated with certain chemotherapy regimens, bone marrow transplants are given as a means to restore bone marrow functioning and immunity after chemotherapy treatment.

Bone marrow transplants can come from a related or unrelated donor, or from the patients themselves. For instance, in some women with metastatic breast cancer, bone marrow can be obtained before chemotherapy treatment and stored frozen. The woman then receives potentially lethal doses of chemotherapy. Once the maximal amount of chemotherapy has been delivered, her frozen bone marrow can be thawed and injected to restore bone marrow functioning. This approach has improved anticancer therapy for some patients.

Bone marrow transplantation has also been successfully used in a number of inherited disorders that affect the ability of the bone marrow to function properly. In this case, bone marrow is taken from related individuals who have similar tissue types to minimize the risk of transplant rejection. The first successful transplant in this situation was performed in a child with severe combined immunodeficiency (SCID) in 1968.

Advances in gene therapy will significantly alter the need for bone marrow transplantation. The primary shift will be from using bone marrow from relatives or unrelated individuals to using the patient's own bone marrow that is genetically corrected. Using the patient's bone marrow is advantageous, eliminating the risk of rejection and graft-versus-host disease. As a consequence, bone marrow transplantation when combined with gene therapy will become a more broadly applicable treatment for a variety of human diseases. The first example of this was reported in the spring of 2000 in patients with SCID who were successfully treated with gene transfer into bone marrow cells, restoring immunity without the need for administering bone marrow from another individual.[6]

Bone marrow transplantation combined with gene therapy is ethically attractive. Bone marrow transplantation is even more accepted and appealing than solid-organ transplantation because one is removing a renewable source from the donor. Like donating blood at the blood bank, the removal of bone marrow cells from the donor is only a temporary loss, as the body replenishes the donated bone marrow cells in a short period of time. The continued use of bone marrow for therapy is expected for a variety of conditions with increasing application of genetic modifications to the bone marrow cells.

MONOCLONAL ANTIBODIES

The "mono" in *monoclonal antibodies* refers to the fact that these antibodies are designed to bind to only one protein. This protein may be on the surface of a cell, inside it, or circulating in the blood. The potential uses of monoclonal antibodies are wide-ranging, indeed.[7] For instance, they could be used selectively to target viruses, bacteria, fungi, cancer cells, drugs, poisons, or other disease-producing cells in order to delete them from the body. Monoclonal antibodies were first developed in the 1970s, but for a variety of technical reasons monoclonal antibody therapies have required a significant amount

6. M. Cavazzana-Calvo, S. Hacein-Bey, B. G. de Saint, F. Gross, E. Yvon, P. Nusbaum, F. Selz, C. Hue, S. Certain, J. L. Casanova, P. Bousso, F. L. Deist, and A. Fischer, "Gene Therapy of Human Severe Combined Immunodeficiency (SCID)-X1 Disease," *Science*, 288 (2000): 669-672.

7. F.C. Breedveld, "Therapeutic Monoclonal Antibodies," *Lancet*, 26 (2000): 735-740.

of time in research before reaching routine clinical practice. The FDA approved the first application of monoclonal antibodies for breast cancer therapy in 1998. This new drug, Herceptin, targets an epidermal growth factor receptor 2 protein called HER2 that is found in large quantities on the surface of 25–30 percent of primary breast cancers.[8] Increased HER2 protein production occurs when tumor cells increase the number of HER2 genes they contain. "Gene amplification," as this is known, is one component of the process through which cells become malignant and maintain their malignant features. Studies in patients have demonstrated that women with HER2 gene amplification have a significantly increased risk of metastasis and require unusually aggressive therapy at diagnosis to prevent recurrence of the cancer. So in order to know when to implement Herceptin therapy, a physician must determine who has too many HER2 genes, and that requires the use of a genetic diagnostic test that needed separate FDA approval.[9] This is the first example of an FDA-approved combination of monoclonal antibody treatment with a genetic assay for guiding cancer therapy.

Understanding the genetic basis of disease can lead to diagnostic tests that allow physicians to select the optimal drug specifically to target the tumor cells. What this means in practice is that the breast cancer patient has the usual biopsy of the tumor. But in addition to the standard tests on tumor tissue, a HER2 genetic test is performed. In women who have a positive HER2 assay, Herceptin is then added to the treatment regimen. Since Herceptin is a monoclonal antibody that is directed specifically to one protein found on cancer cells, the treatment is not associated with many of the undesirable side

---

8. J. Baselga, L. Norton, J. Albanell, Y.-M. Kim, and J. Mendelsohn, "Recombinant Humanized Anti-HER2 Antibody (Herceptin™) Enhances the Antitumor Activity of Paclitaxel and Doxorubicin against HER2/*neu* Overexpressing Human Breast Cancer Xenografts," *Cancer Research*, 58 (1998): 2825-2831.

9. M. Fiche, H. Avet-Loiseau, M.F. Heymann, F. Moussaly, C. Digabel, M. Joubert, J.M. Classe, F. Dravet, P. Fumoleau, J. Ross, and C.M. Maugard, "Genetic Alterations in Early-Onset Invasive Breast Carcinomas: Correlation of c-erbB-2 Amplification Detected by Fluorescence in situ Hybridization with p53 Accumulation and Tumor Phenotype," *International Journal of Cancer*, 84 (1999): 511-515.

effects found with traditional chemotherapy that targets all rapidly dividing cells.

As I think about the ethics of these developments, I would say that the use of monoclonal antibodies for therapy is very similar to small-molecule drug therapies. The association of a genetic assay with a monoclonal antibody or small-molecule drug treatment begins to merge the newest genetic technologies with the older, more typical treatments. This is very important and will lead to markedly improved therapies that are both safer and more effective. I expect that we will see many more monoclonal antibody therapies such as Herceptin on the market this decade.

SOMATIC CELL GENE THERAPY (GENE TRANSFER)

Genes tell cells how to make proteins. If a gene's instructions are incorrect, its protein may be missing or defective, and this can cause disease. Gene transfer therapy tries to correct this by inserting a correct gene to replace the function of the abnormal gene. The primary goal here is to generate missing proteins in patients whose genetic mutation causes a loss of protein function. This strategy may someday be applied to common genetic disorders like cystic fibrosis (CF) and hemophilia B. It may also be possible to add a new gene to the cell conferring a new function, such as to protect the cell against the toxic side effects of chemotherapy or to immunize it to prevent infection.

Gene transfer may also play an especially prominent role in the future of immunizations. Current vaccines and immunizations typically contain killed bacteria or viruses. In contrast, gene therapy immunizations will inject only the relevant genes from various microorganisms. For example, the direct injection of genes from several influenza viruses into animals has induced protective immunity. This occurs because the skin or muscle injected with the viral genes uses the genes to express proteins from the viral genes, mimicking an influenza infection and inducing the desired immune response.[10] Since genes common to different viruses can be simultaneously

---

10. J.B. Ulmer, J. J. Donnelly, S. E. Parker, G.H. Rhodes, P.L. Felgner, V.J. Dwarki, S.H. Gromkowski, R.R. Deck, C.M. DeWitt, and A. Friedman, "Heterologous Protection against Influenza by Injection of DNA Encoding a Viral Protein," *Science*, 259 (1993): 1745-1749.

injected, a single influenza virus gene transfer immunization may be able to protect against a number of viral strains. If successful, this feature would eliminate the need to manufacture a new influenza immunization each year for new strains of the virus. Over the next decade, gene transfer will continue to mature into a clinical therapy for a number of disorders. As of the year 2000, more than five thousand patients have participated in gene therapy experiments worldwide. The safety profile has been remarkably good, but the efficacy has been limited in most patients. In part, this has been related to the fact that most trials are conducted in patients who are debilitated by their disease processes and have been heavily pretreated with other therapies that damage and scar tissues, so they are less likely to respond to these new therapies. However, recent successes using gene transfer for the treatment of SCID and hemophilia B are very promising.[11] Nevertheless, while gene transfer may be turning the corner in its ability effectively to treat inherited genetic disorders, I believe that it will be the new genetic immunizations that will likely be the predominant clinical gene transfer applications in humans, replacing traditional immunization designs.

Most ethicists have pointed out that somatic cell gene transfer is focused on the treatment of one patient, without altering future generations, since alteration of reproductive cells is avoided. Viewed this way, it seems right ethically to think that we are simply using new chemical entities to solve old problems. Instead of injecting insulin from pigs and cattle into patients, we may one day be injecting the insulin gene. Simply using DNA instead of a small-molecule drug to treat a genetic disease has not raised significant new ethical issues.

SOMATIC CELL GENE REPAIR

In addition to transferring genes, it is also possible to repair them. Somatic cell gene repair is the specific correction of a mutation

11. M.A. Kay, C.S. Manno, M.V. Ragni, P.J. Larson, L.B. Couto, A. McClelland, B. Glader, A.J. Chew, S.J. Tai, R. W. Herzog, V. Arruda, F. Johnson, C. Scallan, E. Skarsgard, A.W. Flake, and K.A. High, "Evidence for Gene Transfer and Expression of Factor IX in Haemophilia B Patients Treated with an AAV Vector," *Nature Genetics*, 24 (2000): 257-261.

back to the "normal," also called wild-type, sequence.[12] While mutation correction or repair has been achieved in the laboratory with a number of techniques, it has yet to be tried in humans. Even so, this approach is especially promising for the treatment of dominant disorders where the mutation leads to a disease-causing protein. This includes sickle-cell anemia, which is caused by mutations in the beta-globin gene. As long as the mutated gene is present, it will produce the disease-causing protein. So in this case, simply adding a normal copy of the beta-globin gene may not be very effective. A more compelling strategy is to try to repair the mutation, thereby reducing the disease-causing protein and increasing the normal protein.[13]

Gene repair mutation correction strategies may also be used intentionally to alter the normal DNA sequence to remove a genetic function from a cell. For instance, HIV enters human cells because of normal co-receptors. Perhaps the genetic modification of HIV co-receptors may result in the prevention of HIV infection.[14] While these co-receptors have known cellular functions, no genetic disorders have been definitely associated with these chemokine receptor mutations in individuals born with them, but these individuals seem to resist HIV. Should this mutation be introduced into others? This unusual approach to gene inactivation has not been attempted in humans for HIV infection or any other condition.

Over the next decade, gene repair techniques will mature, just as gene transfer techniques have over the past decade. At this point, the primary problem facing gene repair is low efficiency, not safety. There is a safety advantage built into the process by which gene

12. K.W. Culver, W.-T. Hsieh, Y. Huyen, V. Chen, J. Liu, Y. Khripine, and A. Khorlin, "Correction of Chromosomal Point Mutations in Human Cells with Bifunctional Oligonucleotides," *Nature Biotechnology,* 17 (1999): 989-993.

13. A. Cole-Strauss, K. Yoon, Y. Xiang, B.C. Byrne, M.C. Rice, J. Gryn, W.K. Holloman, and E.B. Kmiec, "Correction of the Mutation Responsible for Sickle Cell Anemia by an RNA- DNA Oligonucleotide," *Science,* 273 (1996): 1386-1389.

14. L.G. Kostrikis, Y. Huang, J.P. Moore, S.M. Wolinsky, L. Zhang, Y. Guo, L. Deutsch, J. Phair, A.U. Neumann, and D.D. Ho, "A Chemokine Receptor CCR2 Allele Delays HIV-1 Disease Progression and Is Associated with a CCR5 Promoter Mutation," *Nature Medicine,* 4 (1998): 350-353.

repair is achieved. Gene repair uses what are called oligonucleotides to induce the cell's own DNA repair machinery to repair the mutation. The oligonucleotides change the DNA in cells but leave no extraneous material behind, unlike gene transfer techniques. This markedly improved safety profile will probably make this the preferred method for use in germ line modifications, nuclear transfer, and stem cell experiments.

Like somatic cell gene transfer, somatic cell gene repair raises no major new ethical issues. In fact, I would argue that limiting the development of these technologies or preventing their development is unethical.

Stem Cell Transplants

In 1998, a number of researchers were successful in growing human stem cells from embryonic and fetal tissues.[15] Stem cells by definition are "multipotential," meaning that they have the potential to grow into a variety of different types of cells.[16] Therefore, treatments using stem cells may allow the growth of cells that can repair damaged nervous tissue in the spinal cord, replace damaged muscle after a heart attack, replace brain cells lost in Parkinson's disease, or replace lost insulin-producing cells in type I diabetes mellitus. The replacement of lost cells such as these is not possible with current technologies discussed earlier in this chapter. The prospect of these applications of human stem cell transplantation is very exciting for medicine.

It is my expectation that stem cell transplantation in human beings will begin soon because their potential healing power is so

---

15. J.A. Thomson, J. Itskovitz-Eldor, S.S. Shapiro, M.A. Waknitz, J.J. Swiergiel, V.S. Marshall, and J.M. Jones, "Embryonic Stem Cell Lines Derived from Human Blastocysts," *Science,* 282 (1998): 1145-1147; and M.J. Shamblott, J. Axelman, S.Wang, E.M. Bugg, J.W. Littlefield, P.J. Donovan, P.D. Blumenthal, G.R. Huggins, J.D. Gearhart, "Derivation of Pluripotent Stem Cells from Cultured Human Primordial Germ Cells," *Proceedings of the National Academy of Science of the United States of America,* 95 (1998): 13726-731.

16. G. Vogel. "Can Old Cells Learn New Tricks?" *Science,* 287 (2000): 1418-1419.

great. With proper regulatory oversight, human stem cells should be approved for use in a variety of circumstances, especially those with central nervous system abnormalities. The ethical controversy associated with the potential transplantation of stem cells into the human body is related to the source of these potentially healing cells rather than their use for transplantation.

The original stem cells reported in 1998 were derived from embryos left over from reproductive clinics and from aborted fetuses. Researchers observed standard informed consent procedures, but many object to these sources being used in this way. In the United States, federal funds may not be used for embryo research, and there is a debate over whether or not stem cell work falls into that category. Private research foundations and corporations, however, are allowed to work with discarded human embryos and fetal tissue. As a consequence, the recent identification of human stem cells was delayed for a significant period of time. Discussions are under way within government and scientific bodies to establish a set of criteria that will allow stem cell research to proceed while maintaining proper safeguards for human embryos and aborted fetuses.

Aside from this concern, stem cell technology enjoys strong support, which makes sense given that we have supported the transplantation of organs from other human beings and animals for many years.

GERM LINE GENETIC MODIFICATION

Germ line genetic modification is an appealing treatment strategy for a number of genetic conditions that cause severe, irreversible consequences in utero or lead to spontaneous abortion and/or infertility. The fundamental difference from somatic cell modification is that germ line modification may alter the genes that are passed to offspring and to their descendants indefinitely. The implications of germ line modification are great, and so the margin of safety must be broad before approval is given to germ line modification experiments.

It is my expectation that recent advances in genetic technologies are providing a sound basis for future human applications of intentional germ line modification. The new possibilities for gene repair will likely reduce scientific barriers for human germ line intervention. These new oligonucleotide-based technologies leave no extra DNA, correcting the DNA sequence back to the natural or "wild-type" sequence. Other genes and the cell's regulation of their expression are not disturbed. These features of the oligonucleotide approach are ideal for germ line modification. Another critical scientific achievement has been the development of ways to monitor the effects of gene modification. Gene expression arrays are now available to monitor the intracellular effects of cellular modification.[17] This technology allows the researcher to monitor very closely the gene expression alterations induced by tissue culture conditions, drug treatment, or other medical techniques. This will allow for the optimization of modifications and will facilitate the most likely scenario for success with germ line modification.

When and where germ line modification will begin is difficult to predict. I would expect that the likely place to start human experimentation is in the treatment of nonviable embryos in order to salvage them or to modify spermatogonia cells for the treatment of infertility. In these cases, the moral status of the embryo can be protected and valued by correcting the mutation at that stage to allow for a healthy child, where no child would have otherwise resulted.

I anticipate that it will be a number of years before the gene repair technologies will be judged safe enough for an attempt at human germ line modification. Once safe application in reproductive tissues and embryos has been achieved, however, the choice of which diseases should be targeted for elimination from the gene pool will be a challenging decision.

NUCLEAR TRANSFER AND CLONING

In 1996, scientists in Scotland stunned the world by demonstrating that a nucleus from an adult cell could be used to clone sheep.[18] The creation of Dolly suggested that indeed it might soon be pos-

---

17. R.J. Lipshutz, S.P.A. Fodor, T.R. Gingeras, and D.J. Lockhart, "High Density Synthetic Oligonucleotide Arrays," *Nature Genetics*, 21 (1999): 20-24.

18. K.H. Campbell, J. McWhir, W.A. Ritchie, and I. Wilmut, "Sheep Cloned by Nuclear Transfer from a Cultured Cell Line," *Nature*, 380 (1996): 64-66.

sible routinely to clone mammals. The scientists who created Dolly, Polly, and Molly tried more than two hundred times to create the one cloned sheep Dolly. Subsequent to that significant achievement, investigators around the world have cloned goats, mice, cattle, pigs, and monkeys.[19,20]

The question arises as to the circumstances under which cloning a human being would be appropriate. In my opinion, it is scientifically inappropriate with current techniques even to consider trying to clone a human due to the limitations of existing technologies. However, with years of additional research, technology may become available, as it eventually will for germ line modification, that may theoretically allow the cloning of humans. Many reasons for and against the cloning of human beings have been put forth. It is difficult for me at this time to identify a compelling circumstance for which human cloning would be appropriate.

However, nuclear transfer may well be appropriate for patients who suffer from mitochondrial disorders. Mitochondria are intracellular DNA structures outside the nucleus. When the DNA in mitochondria is mutant, the patients may suffer from one of a variety of inherited disorders. An ovum from a woman with mutant mitochondria can have her nuclear DNA taken out of it and transferred into another cell with normal mitochondria that has the nucleus removed. The resulting cell is then fertilized with the father's sperm to begin an embryo. This type of nuclear transfer is also known as IVONT (in vitro ovum nuclear transplantation).[21] This

19. A. Baguisi, E. Behboodi, D.T. Melican, J.S. Pollock, M.M. Destrempes, C. Cammuso, J.L. Williams, S.D. Nims, C.A. Porter, P. Midura, M.J. Palacios, S.L. Ayres, R.S. Denniston, M.L. Hayes, C.A. Ziomek, H.M. Meade, R.A. Godke, W.G. Gavin, E.W. Overström, and Y. Echelard, "Production of Goats by Somatic Cell Nuclear Transfer," *Nature Biotechnology,* 17 (1999): 456-461.

20. T. Wakayama, I. Rodriguez, A.C.F. Perry, R. Yanagimachi, and P. Mombaerts, "Mice Cloned from Embryonic Stem Cells," *Proceedings of the National Academy of Science of the United States of America,* 96 (1999): 14984-989.

21. D.S. Rubenstein, D.C. Thomasma, E.A. Schon, and M.J. Zinaman. "Response to Germ-Line Therapy to Cure Mitochondrial Disease: Protocol and Ethics of in vitro Ovum Nuclear Transplantation," *Cambridge Quarterly of Healthcare Ethics,* 5 (1996): 450-457.

approach does not give rise to clones but does offer a way to treat mitochondrial disorders. In this case, the maternal cell used for fertilization would have the mother's nucleus and all of her chromosomes, while the mitochondria would be from the donor. We can see here that nuclear transfer and cloning are not synonymous.

It is my expectation that over time, nuclear transfer technologies will become efficient, safe, and reliable. Nuclear transfer technologies will offer us the ability to create stem cells as well as treat mitochondrial disorders.[22] This is advantageous over using established stem cell lines grown from unrelated embryos because modified cell lines are expected to be fully compatible with the patient and therefore not rejected by the patient's immune system. It will be these types of uses that will solve a variety of the remaining health challenges. Nuclear transfer, in conjunction with other techniques, will render human cloning irrelevant to the treatment of human disease.

CONCLUSION

There is no doubt that genetics is revolutionizing every aspect of medical practice. From the development of diagnostic tests and the design of small-molecule drugs to genetic therapies, the way diseases will be diagnosed and treated in the future will be vastly different from today. This is of great value and hope for those who suffer from a variety of disorders. Understanding the genetic basis of disease allows the development of drugs or genetic therapies that will target the fundamental basis of the disease, eliminating all of the symptoms. This is well beyond the scope of current medical practice, but it is the hope that guides today's research.

It is even possible that small-molecule drugs may be used to cure genetic disorders by transiently inhibiting or replacing certain genetic processes that lead to malformations of organs, to the development of malignancy, or for the prevention of infections. This will only be possible due to an understanding of the genetic basis of disease. It is genetic therapies that offer the long-term cures dreamed of by patients, families, and physicians. Somatic cell

22. J.B. Gurdon and A. Colman, "The Future of Cloning," *Nature*, 402 (2000): 743-746.

gene transfer and gene repair technologies will mature in time into viable clinical therapies, offering enormous benefit to patients. Success with somatic cell genetic modification will inevitably lead to an increasing desire to manipulate the germ line to eliminate severe disorders from the gene pool. The advent of germ line genetic modification, whether by gene transfer, gene repair, or nuclear transfer, will require major advances in technology, extensive open public dialogue, and the identification of clinical disorders that truly can only be benefited with germ line modification, such as male infertility. Successful application of the germ line modification for rare diseases will raise even more difficult questions regarding potential application to common disorders. It is important that public dialogue continues in anticipation of reaching technological feasibility during the next several decades.

Overall, the advances made in the understanding of the genetic basis of disease and the ability to repair genetic abnormalities have created the most exciting period ever in biomedical research and clinical medicine. Never before have we had the potential not only to treat the fundamental basis of the disease but to prevent the onset of illnesses. As a Christian physician-scientist, I am confident that the goals of these new genetic treatments of human disease are absolutely consistent with the compassionate example and the teachings of Jesus Christ, who used extraordinary powers in his ministry to heal the fundamental bases of illness.

---------------------- 3 ----------------------

Ethics Keeping Pace with Technology

Donald M. Bruce

*From his office in Edinburgh, Scotland, Donald Bruce has had
a ringside seat as the cloning controversy has unfolded. Even
before Dolly became a household world, he was engaging with
Ian Wilmut and others at Roslyn Institute in Edinburgh on the
ethics of animal cloning and possible human applications.
Bruce tells the story of the engagement of the churches in
Europe in the public discussions of stem cells, cloning, and other
forms of biotechnology, reminding us that Christian ethics not
only can keep up with technology, but that it must do so.*

Dolly the cloned sheep has become one of the icons of the turn of
the millennium. She has a characteristically postmodern ambivalence, symbolizing simultaneously the hopes and the fears about
where biotechnological research has brought us. She also marks
the globalization of bioethics in the age of instant worldwide com-
munications. For the first time in history, there was an immediate,
worldwide moral reaction that human technology should not proceed to do something it might be able to do. Postmodernity ironically found itself facing a near universal ethical judgment as
bioethics faced the global media.

When reporters descended on Roslin Institute outside
Edinburgh in February, 1997, local photographer Murdo MacLeod
took the photograph of Dolly, who is indeed a remarkably friendly
animal, apparently holding court to a herd of paparazzi. The photograph makes an astute social comment. Mammalian nuclear transfer, far from being arcane, is a Pavlovian prompt for the media to
rush after the scent of a new story. In the United Kingdom, perhaps

more than elsewhere, cloning is news in a way that equally far-reaching developments over the same period in stem cell technology and gene patenting are not. As with the genetically modified food debate, cloning provokes a question about the power of the media to determine what are seen as public issues in bioethics and how they are discussed in civil society.

Cloning now possesses an aura of mystery. Having set it up to be so, reporters seemingly cannot wait to report the scandal of the first human clone. But in reality, such obsession with human cloning is something of a diversion from the directions in which cloning technology itself has been going since 1995, when the first cloned sheep, Megan and Morag, were produced from cultured embryo cells. The technology has taken three distinct paths from there. One led to Dolly, born in 1996 and introduced to the world in February 1997. She was the remarkable proof that it is possible, albeit inefficient, to clone a mammal from adult, somatic cells. The second occurred in July, 1997, when Polly and three siblings were born, repeating cloning but with fetal cells that had been genetically modified by the insertion of a human gene, for the expression of human blood clotting factor IX. This represented the first time that a large genetically modified animal had been "grown" from cultured cells, and this was the original aim of Roslin's cloning work. A third path was the extension of cloning techniques to other mammals, including cattle, goats, mice, and pigs, at Roslin and other labs around the world.

While these breakthroughs have been occurring in the field of mammalian cloning, the public attitude in Europe toward technology has been undergoing a profound shift, beginning with nuclear energy and growing with the awareness of global environmental threats like the ozone hole and climate change. In the United Kingdom, the failure of regulators to avoid the Bovine Spongiform Encephalopathy ("mad cow") crisis, and to take seriously public concerns over genetically modified food, has sown further doubt about modern technological projects. With this doubt there has emerged a rival attitude that equates "natural" with "good" and sees human intervention with increasing skepticism. This exaltation of the natural is in response to the perception that technology has overreached itself into areas where human wisdom has not accompanied human ingenuity.

Christians should not endorse this view uncritically, but should be mindful of an important tension that exists between the first and second accounts of creation in the book of Genesis. In Genesis 1, strong language of dominion is used, and human beings are commanded to "subdue the earth and fill it," to "rule over" the rest of God's creation, as befits the raw elemental character of nature in that account. In Genesis 2, however, creation is represented in the softer metaphor of a garden, which humans are to "work and care for." Here is found a creative tension of human intervention moderated by a more relational outlook. While the current secular trend may be said to reflect something of this moderating stance of Genesis 2, it lacks the biblical counterpoint of Genesis 1 to restrain it from going too far and becoming an alternative view, shifting into a pagan concept of nature as inherently sacred. A Christian view cannot simply replace one metaphor with the other, but seeks to find a dynamic balance, giving due credit to the divine calling for human beings to intervene in nature as well as the need to conserve and respect it.

While these technical developments and public shifts were occurring, I have been in close contact with the researchers at Roslin. I also serve on a European church working group on bioethics, which offered this theological preamble to its statement about cloning:

> It is inherent in our nature to find ways to shape the created order around us. When we speak of creation, however, this should not be read as if it were a single event, but includes the continuous evolutionary unfolding of the natural order, of which God is both author and sustainer. Indeed, when the ancient Genesis account describes humans bearing the "image of God" and naming the animals, something creative is implied. As Christians, therefore we are certainly not opposed to biotechnology or biomedical research as such. We are conscious, however, not every development is necessarily acceptable, and that we need to critique the impulses which drive biotechnology and which set its priorities. We have undoubtedly seen important progress in recent years. We have gained a much better understanding of the mechanisms that control many of the processes of life. Yet the more powerful the methods we use, the more we need to consider not only what is technically possible,

but what is happening to us as people if we say "yes" to every possibility which science may enable. The drive to "see if we can do it" which seems at times to be the primary propelling force needs better channeling. Molecular biology is in many ways an immature science. It has begun to realize its power, but has not found out how to use that power in balance with wider aspects of life, and with a realistic understanding of human nature.

Our Christian heritage teaches us to be skeptical of romantic notions of unrestrained human improvement and scientific progress that prevail in some parts of the scientific and political communities. Our support for scientific research is moderated by our awareness of human finiteness and fallibility. We do not know as much about biology as we sometimes think, and human nature sadly inclines us to misuse our God-given talents as well as to use them well. The Bible teaches a holistic view of human life, fulfilled in relationship. Respect for the human person and for our relationships with each other and with the rest of God's creation are therefore more important criteria than mere progress, economic well being, or medical advance in themselves. Good though these things can be, they are not absolutes. This leads us to the conclusion that not all technical progress in biotechnology is necessarily desirable. To become mature, it must learn where to say "no", as well as "yes". This is especially so with cloning.[1]

From this theological perspective, an ethical case is made that human reproductive cloning must be considered intrinsically wrong, and the dilemmas involved in nonreproductive or therapeutic applications are also assessed.

REPRODUCTIVE HUMAN CLONING

Perhaps the most striking feature of the immediate and continuing public reaction in the United Kingdom, Europe, and indeed much of the world has been the widespread intuition that cloning is inherently wrong. In predominantly secularized cultures, it was ironic to see the expression "playing God" used to express the idea

1. Executive Committee of the European Ecumenical Commission for Church and Society (EECCS), "Cloning Animals and Humans: An Ethical View," Strasbourg, May 1998.

not just that humans were intervening too far into nature, but violating some sense of an absolute moral norm. It was, however, unclear in the early pronouncements of various committees just what moral norm was threatened.

Article 11 of the UNESCO Universal Declaration on Human Genome Rights simply states, "Practices which are contrary to human dignity, such as reproductive cloning of human beings, shall not be permitted."[2] The European Parliament resolution advanced a variety of reasons to oppose cloning: "The cloning of human beings...cannot be justified or tolerated by any society, because it is a serious violation of human rights and is contrary to the principle of equality of human beings as it permits a eugenic and racist selection of the human race, it offends against human dignity and it requires experimentation on human beings."[3] The concepts of human rights or dignity were evoked without elaboration, however. Whatever such rhetoric may achieve in a public declaration or legal instrument, it does not automatically constitute an ethical case. For instance, arguments based on rights are problematical in Christian theology, and, in the United States, also draw one into discussion over opposing rights, such as the right to reproduce.

The Church of Scotland[4, 5] and the European churches working group[6] examined a number of possible approaches to the case that human reproductive cloning is wrong in principle and reached the conclusion that arguments from unnaturalness, playing God, and genetic diversity were all insufficient to sustain a case against

2. United Nations Educational, Scientific and Cultural Organization, "Universal Declaration on the Human Genome and Human Rights," Paris, November 11, 1997, Article11.

3. European Parliament, "Resolution on Cloning," Strasbourg, March 12,1997, Clause B.

4. "Cloning Animals and Humans," Supplementary Reports to the Church of Scotland General Assembly, May, 1997, p. 36/22, and Board of National Mission deliverances 35 and 36, p.16.

5. Donald M. Bruce, "Cloning Issues in Reproduction, Science and Medicine, A Submission to the Human Genetics Advisory Commission and Human Fertilisation and Embryology Authority," May 7, 1998, Society, Religion and Technology Project, Church of Scotland, Edinburgh.

6. EECCS, "Cloning Animals," ibid.

reproductive cloning. The argument that cloning is absolutely unnatural fails in scientific terms because cloning is a fairly common phenomenon among plants and microorganisms. If one buries a potato in the ground, a clone is produced. There are also some examples in the animal kingdom of what amounts naturally to cloning, but mammals or human beings reproduce only sexually. The biological distinction between sexual and asexual reproduction raises a most pertinent question. Should humans respect this biological distinction, or should we exult in our human capacity to override such limitations? The argument shifts from one that cloning is unnatural to asking what aspects of nature is it appropriate for humans to change.

One seeks in vain for a biblical warrant that would declare human or animal cloning forbidden territory, simply on the ground that as human beings we would overreach ourselves and our divine calling. "Playing God" can be an expression of divine prohibition, but it can also be considered an expression of God's calling to humanity to assume a priestly role on God's behalf toward and within the rest of creation. We are to act in a Godlike way in an imaginative, caring, and creative development of the created order.

Human reproductive cloning, I believe, is wrong because of more particular reasons associated with the character of what cloning entails. Cloning represents a departure from the overall course of sexual reproduction, so that instead of creating an entirely new genetic individual it replicates an existing one. This might be said to be a step in the wrong direction, both theologically and genetically—genetically, in regard to the diversity needed by a healthy population and theologically, in regard to one of the most celebrated characteristics of God's creative activity.[7] The phenomenon of identical twins argues against the notion that genetic identity is in itself wrong. What cloning does, however, is to put such power into human hands, and herein lies the real issue, that of control.

---

7. Donald M. Bruce, "A View from Edinburgh," in Ronald Cole-Turner, editor, *Human Cloning: Religious Responses* (Louisville, Ky.: Westminster John Knox Press, 1997), 1-11.

Twinning is a random, unpredictable event. It involves the duplicating of a genetic composition but one that has never existed before and which at that point is unknown to anyone. Cloning, however, would choose the genetic composition of some existing person and make another individual with the same genes. It is thus an intentional, controlled action to produce a specific known end. It means that the entire genetic composition of a new individual is not random but has been chosen, controlled, and predetermined by another human being. It is this act of human control, I believe, that makes human reproductive cloning inherently wrong. It is not for humans to predetermine the exact genetics of other humans.

By control, one certainly does not mean that through genetic control every characteristic of the new person is thereby prefigured. Christians would be among the first to refute such crude genetic determinism. The biblical picture of humanity is a holistic notion of being, which in modern terms embraces genes, environment, and the relational and spiritual dimensions of existence. Yet the money and skill invested in the human genome project bears testimony to how important we consider our genes to be. Genes also differ from environment or nurture in one vital sense. Notwithstanding all that parents, friends, educators, and governments may do to direct a child's upbringing into this or that direction, these can never be absolutely determinative. In principle, each of us can reject any aspect of our upbringing, but once born we cannot change our genetic complement. That is irreversible. To engage in human cloning would mean unprecedented control by some individuals over the genetic inheritance of others. People tend to be critical of parents or social institutions if they attempt to direct a child unduly. How much more is this the case with the power completely to predetermine the child's *genes*. Such control by one human being over another is incompatible with the ethical notion of human freedom, in the sense of that each individual's genetic identity should be inherently unpredictable and unplanned.

Our science cannot claim omniscience. Indeed, in the biblical understanding, our wisdom and discernment are profoundly disfigured by the moral collapse resulting from human defiance and the assertion of autonomy over against our proper relationship with God. To use the powers inherent in human cloning would be to open a Pandora's box psychologically and in terms of family relationships. No one knows what it is like to discover that one is the genetic copy of one's father or mother, a twin but removed by a generation, nor indeed how this knowledge would affect the parents' behavior. We might expect that these effects will vary from person to person, but there are sufficient dangers to apply the precautionary principle. There is a serious risk of dysfunctional persons and relationships emerging by the inherent nature of the technique, beyond those that exist in normal reproduction. There can be no reliable way ever to predict the outcome. Consequently, it is wrong knowingly to inflict that risk on one who is in no position to consent.

In practical terms, human reproductive cloning is extremely, indeed criminally foolhardy, on the present evidence of the serious welfare problems arising in animal cloning in most species so far attempted. For this reason, Ian Wilmut has publicly criticized anyone who would attempt it, and the United Kingdom authorities are similarly unequivocal in their opposition. The inherent uncertainties in nuclear transfer cell reprogramming seem unlikely to be overcome sufficiently to justify ethically the risk of producing severely deformed babies. No animal experiment will provide sufficient assurance. We cannot test the risk without running the risk.

THERAPEUTIC APPLICATIONS OF HUMAN CLONING

The primary focus of nuclear transfer cloning research has shifted to human therapeutic purposes, in conjunction with the new discoveries in human stem cell technology. Skin or blood cells might be taken from someone suffering from a degenerative disease like Parkinson's, for instance, and fused with an enucleated human egg to produce a cloned embryo. Instead of being implanted to produce a new person, the cloned embryo would serve as a source of stem cells, which would then be programmed to produce nerve cells for treating the disease. Such cells could also be produced from "spare" embryos from IVF treatment, but cloned embryos would reduce the risk of rejection by the immune system, because, unlike IVF embryos, cloned embryos would be of the patient's own genes.

Recent developments suggest that stem cells derived from adult tissue, and not involving the use of embryos at all, are capable of generating many different cell types. This is certainly an option to be given the highest research priority, but we should be cautious before assuming adult-derived cells would have the full range of applications that are expected of embryonic stem cells.

These applications are a long way from being practicable. There is a formidable list of experimental hurdles to overcome in each case. No one knows how successful stem cell therapies would be clinically, nor what risk there is of cultured cells becoming cancerous.[8] We may prematurely raise expectations among those suffering from these diseases. Compared with reproductive cloning, these developments raise different and equally searching ethical questions. Following the recommendations of the Donaldson Report, the United Kingdom Parliament voted by a large majority to allow research on human embryos "for the understanding of serious diseases," including the creation of embryonic stem cells. It also allows the creation of cloned human embryos for this purpose.[9] These are both highly controversial outcomes.

Earlier in the same year, the European churches bioethics group has responded to the Donaldson Report with the following insights,[10] derived and modified from the Church of Scotland's work.[11] In the paragraphs that follow, the bioethics groups first takes up the question of whether it is right to destroy an embryo in order to derive stem cells.

8. Philip Cohen, "Hold the Champagne," *New Scientist*, November 1998, 6.

9. The Chief Medical Officer's Expert Group, Department of Health, The United Kingdom, *Stem Cell Research: Medical Progress with Responsibility*, London, June 2000.

10. Bioethics Working Group of the Church and Society Commission of the Conference of European Churches, Therapeutic Uses of Cloning and Embryonic Stem Cells—A Discussion Paper, conference of European Churches (Strasbourg, September 2000).

11. Church of Scotland, "Submission to the Chief Medical Officer's Expert Group on Cloning," Society, Religion and Technology Project and the Board of Social Responsibility, Church of Scotland, Edinburgh, October 1999.

To find treatments for diseases like Parkinson's and diabetes would be a very desirable outcome. This is not sufficient cause to justify the application automatically, without first assessing the intrinsic issues of the use of the embryo that would be involved in the proposed research and therapies. Thus, before evaluating the consequences of embryo use, there is a prior question that must be asked. Is the proposed research something we should not be *doing* to the embryo itself, no matter what diseases were to be treated? We rightly recoil at the idea of killing a human being in order to provide spare parts or cells for another. Should we use an early embryo to provide the cells? National legislation and perspectives vary across Europe, reflecting the deep ethical conflicts that exist about the nature of the embryo. This conflict may be summarized approximately as beliefs at two opposite poles and various intermediate viewpoints.

One extreme sees the early embryo as a ball of cells and nothing more. Because it is undeveloped and would not survive out of the womb, research on human embryos is permissible, and they may also be used routinely as a source of stem cells. The potential medical consequences wholly justify the action.

The other pole is that from conception onwards the embryo has the status of humanity, allowing no research or use that was not for the benefit of that particular embryo. This rejects any technology that involves creating dispensable embryos, including the provision of replacement cells. Many Christians take the view that once God creates life, even in embryo, it is not for humans to destroy it. This is a matter of principle, regardless of the application. Those holding this position would advocate only the use of stem cells or replacement that were derived from adult tissue. Any use that involved embryos would be ethically impermissible.

An example of an intermediate position is that of the Church of Scotland General Assembly, which considered a range of embryological issues in 1996.[12] It affirmed the sanctity of the human embryo from conception but granted that there were limited circumstances under which such research might reluctantly be allowed prior to the "primitive streak" stage, bearing in mind the seriousness of certain medical conditions. These were primarily seen as infertility and

12. Church of Scotland, "Pre-Conceived Ideas," Report of the Board of Social Responsibility to the 1996 General Assembly of the Church of Scotland (Edinburgh: St. Andrew Press, 1996).

genetically transmitted diseases. The question posed to such an intermediate position is this. Does the proposed embryonic stem cell research and cell replacement therapy fall within existing ethical categories or does it represent an ethical step change in the use of the embryo?

To the extent that this position may allow embryo research for some limited purposes, a measure of instrumentality towards the embryo has been accepted. The question is then whether this constitutes an allowance for all instrumental uses, or only some. However, taking the applications currently allowed in the UK context as an example, it may be argued that in most of these the embryo is being treated as an entity in itself. The difference with the proposed new research is that it seems to reduce the embryo to becoming a mere resource from which convenient parts, in this case cells, are taken.

It might be said that an early embryo is potentially all the cells of the human body, and therefore one is not destroying it, but merely directing it to become certain cells and not others. The concern, however, is that by the same token the embryo is prevented from developing in its normal complete fashion. By forcing the embryo to become only a certain type of cell, it is prevented from becoming all the cells as a whole. It is not "taking a cutting" from the embryo, but completely reprogramming it. This would be a profound ethical change in what is considered right about the embryo. It would drive the present ambiguity of the intermediate position over the status of the embryo down the side of being a "ball of cells." It would drive it much further away from its connection with a delivered baby.

The current UK legislation upholds a principle from the 1984 Warnock Report that the embryo should be accorded "a special status."[13] Although the notion was ill defined, it is hard to see how the embryo would retain any "special status" if it were now merely a convenient resource for replacement cells. The new proposals would seem to go a significant step further in treating the early embryo *only* as a means to an end.

Thus we conclude that what is envisaged would be a profound ethical change in what is considered right about the embryo. To

---

13. Ministry of Health, *Report of the Committee of Inquiry in Human Fertilisation and Embryology* (Warnock Report), Her Majesty's Stationery Office, London, 1984.

allow the use of embryos for this purpose therefore would need to follow a purely utilitarian argument. This is indeed what the Donaldson report ultimately does. It asserts that it is "not lacking in respect" towards the moral status of the embryo, provided they are used to secure benefits to human health. It suggests that if the potential benefit of treating terminal illness is arguably greater than treating infertility, then the new proposals could actually confer a greater respect for the embryo because of the nobler purpose for which it is being used (4.10). This argument sees the embryo just as a means to an end, but now sees greater potential ends from the same means.

However, in 1998 a UK Ministry of Agriculture report into animal cloning stresses that animals have intrinsic value. While we may use them for many purposes, some uses should never be allowed.[14] It cautioned against seeing animals "merely as means to an end." It would seem strange indeed at a time when animal experimentation is increasingly being brought into question, the use of human embryos seems to be much more acceptable. We should be cautious of treating human embryos with less respect than animals.[15]

The European churches bioethics group turns next to a second difficult question, whether it is permissible to use cloning to create an embryo, not for implantation, but for the purposes of deriving stem cells for therapy.

Firstly, it seems illogical to allow the creation of a cloned human embryo knowing full well one would have to destroy it on *ethical* grounds, because it was unethical to allow it to go to term to produce a cloned baby. The second objection is that this involves the deliberate creation of an embryo for other than reproductive purposes, although this is not specific to cloning. The use of "spare" embryos from fertility treatments would be a use of an embryo that would be destroyed anyway.

---

14. Farm Animal Welfare Council, *Report on the Implications of Cloning for the Welfare of Cloned Livestock*, PB 4132, Ministry of Agriculture, Fisheries and Food, London, 1998.

15. Bioethics Working Group of the Church and Society Commission of the Conference of European Churches, "Therapeutic Uses of Cloning and Embryonic Stem Cells: A Discussion Paper" (Strasbourg, September 2000).]

Thirdly, there is a gradualism argument. Once cloned human embryos were created, it would be much easier for someone misguided enough to go the next step and allow them to be implanted, or for someone rich enough to seek a clandestine "off-shore" treatment. This underlines the need for clear national laws, in those states which do not currently have them, to outlaw the practice of human cloning worldwide.

The creation and use of cloned embryos should not be allowed as a general therapeutic procedure. We urge, however, that a priority should be put on nuclear transfer research which aims at avoiding use of embryos, by direct programming from one adult body tissue type to another. One could take, perhaps, a blood sample and reprogram directly into becoming, say, a set of nerve cells. This is of course even more speculative than the methods discussed above, but several routes have recently been suggested. Ethically this would remove most of the above objections.

There is also a further reason. The ethics committee of Roslin's collaborators, the Geron Biomed company, has urged that the technique should have the widest applicability and not be simply a treatment for the rich. It is very unlikely that enough human donor eggs could ever be provided to treat the millions of potential patients across Europe. It would therefore probably be essential to find a method of producing replacement cells without using embryos. On present evidence, however, this would probably be impossible without some human embryo research to work out the method. This poses a deep ethical dilemma whether a very limited and fixed number of experiments should be allowed to obtain the data necessary to avoid any such use of embryos in future. Some would reluctantly argue for very limited research for this sole purpose, but if it seemed unlikely to succeed, then it should stop, and not proceed to use embryos routinely for cell therapies.[16]

Animal Cloning in Medicine and Animal-Human Nuclear Transfer

There has been speculation about whether genetically compatible replacement cells might be achieved by cloning but without using human embryos. One idea put forward by Advanced Cell

16. Ibid.

Technologies is to create a non-viable hybrid embryo by means of nuclear transfer of a human cell into an enucleated cow's egg. An electric current would fuse the two and stimulate the human cell to divide as though it were a human embryo, but one that was not viable.[17] At the blastocyst stage of division, the stem cells would be removed and cultured as human somatic cells. Aside from the formidable technical problems, one would need to be quite sure that the use of a cow's egg as a host for the human cell has no adverse effect on the eventual human cell lines. Even though it avoids the creation of a cloned human embryo, the mixing of human and animal genetic material at such a profound level raises a different and major intrinsic ethical objection.[18]

Since Megan and Morag, animal cloning is mainly focused on new ways of genetically modifying animals. This is illustrated by the recent cloning of 5 piglets by PPL Therapeutics, aimed at combating rejection mechanisms in xenotransplantation, which is the potential use of pig organs in humans. Researchers hope that cloning will enable them for first time to knock out a pig gene that triggers rejection by the human body, as well as inserting human genes more accurately to "humanize" pig organs enough to counter other human defense mechanisms. This requires multiple genetic engineering of a large animal, which is uncharted scientific territory. Xenotransplantation represents a completely different way of using animals from anything humans have done before. To create and destroy a highly intelligent animal, for which many people have a special fondness, in order to remove live organs would normally be an unacceptable intervention in one of God's creatures. It might be justified only if the efficacy in quality and length of life for the patient was very considerable. The requirements are severe, both in overcoming rejection and in ensuring a minimal risk of virus transfer from pigs into the human population.[19]

17. Philip Cohen, "Organs without Donors," *New Scientist*, July 1998, 4-5.

18. The Chief Medical Officer's Expert Group, *Stem Cell Research*, 2.34 and 2.62.

19. Working Group on Genetic Engineering in Non-human Life Forms, Society, Religion and Technology Project, Church of Scotland, "Xeno-transplantation—A Submission to the Department on Health" (Edinburgh, 1995).

CONCLUSIONS

This chapter has argued that the general intuition against reproductive human cloning has a sound ethical basis that lies not in genetic identity as such but in its human control. It should not be in the power of one human to predetermine the genetics of another. Human reproductive cloning would also present unacceptable risks, no matter how much progress might eventually be made to reducing animal welfare problems that currently affect much mammalian cloning.

The cloning of embryos to produce genetically compatible replacement cells for treating degenerative diseases is more complex ethically. For those opposed to embryo research in principle, the objection is total. Even for those who accept some level of use of embryos may find objections to using them merely as resources for spare cells, as a means to an end. Such instrumentality would challenge the special status for the embryo in any meaningful sense. Creating cloned embryos for cell replacements presents problems of inconsistency and gradualism if one is opposed to creating cloned embryos for reproduction. The use of nuclear transfer technology should rather be focused towards cell replacement methods that avoid the use of embryos.

The vote by the United Kingdom Parliament to allow research into embryonic stem cells and therapeutic uses of cloning has been welcomed by the scientific and medical communities, who wish to press ahead, in order not to delay therapies or to lose competitive advantages to other countries. These are not the only considerations, however. While the general public appears to be clear in their opposition to reproductive cloning, they are confused about stem cells and embryo cloning. Given the far-reaching and sensitive nature of these technologies, it is essential that scientists not race ahead of the ethical values and understanding of civil society. This is essential if ethics is to keep pace with technology. As Christians we are called to engage with the technological world, bringing a full range of ethical insights to bear, and mindful of the dual mandate placed upon us in Genesis to intervene in and care for God's creation. From my own experience engaging with policymakers and researchers on behalf of the churches in Scotland, I can say that the ethical and faith dimension is also generally welcomed, provided it is well informed. Moral convictions are indeed affecting the way that cloning technology develops. Our challenge is to continue to keep pace with technological change, bringing informed, rigorous, and faithful moral vision equally to the scientific world and the public arena.

4

Making All Things New?

Eric B. Beresford

What accounts for the strong public denunciation of human cloning, and do the ethical arguments advanced to date do justice to the strength of this reaction? Eric Beresford invites us to dig beneath the standard arguments to revisit the thorny theological question of the human embryo. What is the human embryo and what do we owe it? And what about a clone, who is created without conception? Is a cloned embryo the equal of a conceived embryo? These are difficult questions, and all the more so because the technologies of cloning and stem cells change the very meaning of terms like the embryo. Already, however, public science policy depends on our answers. Can our old opinions about the embryo guide the new technology?

The successful cloning of a sheep by Ian Wilmut and Keith Campbell of Roslin Institute near Edinburgh precipitated a reaction, whose direction might easily have been predicted. The strength and persistence of the reaction, however, took many of us by surprise, and a number of reasons have been advanced for it. The technique was certainly groundbreaking, not just as a technique but as a reversal of basic assumptions about nature itself. The early embryo's seemingly identical cells change or differentiate as they divide into the many types of cells that make up the mature organism, and it had long been assumed that it was not possible to clone mammals from cells that had undergone differentiation. Wilmut and his colleagues overcame that difficulty using a technique called somatic cell nuclear transfer. The nucleus of a differentiated cell, taken in this case from the mammary glands of an older ewe, is transferred into an ovum that has had its own nucleus removed.

The breakthrough is also startling ethically, especially when we begin to think about human applications. For some, human cloning is simply morally repugnant. Leon Kass has been the strongest advocate of the language of repugnance and has placed cloning alongside incest and bestiality. He suggests that in all three cases the act is in itself an adequate ground of a revulsion that goes beyond reasoned argument.[1] He also advised the U.S. National Bioethics Advisory Commission to act "as if the future of humanity may lie in the balance."[2] The Evangelical Fellowship of Canada asserts: "Most Christians, as well as the population at large, find cloning in general, and the cloning of humans in particular, repulsive. Ethical justification for this sentiment must rest on fuller understanding of the biblical principles referred to earlier." Two things are remarkable about this last statement. First, having told us how to construct an ethical justification for revulsion at the thought of cloning in general—through reference to biblical principles—the statement fails to provide such justifications even in the case of human cloning. Second, it assumes that such arguments will inevitably support rather than undermine the revulsion against cloning.

As the cloning debate has progressed, it has proved extraordinarily difficult to give clear reasons for the strength of the reaction. This does not mean that such arguments could not be produced, or that the observed emotions are inappropriate, but it is true that emotions without reasons do not constitute good moral arguments that are capable of supporting adequately informed public policy. On the other hand, recent reflection on the nature and role of ethical theory *suggests* that arguments that do not adequately explain our moral impulses and insights are prima facie suspect.[3] Moral reflection needs to take seriously both the arguments advanced and

1. Leon R. Kass, "The Wisdom of Repugnance," in Leon R. Kass and James Q. Wilson, *The Ethics of Human Cloning* (Washington, D.C.: American Enterprise Institute Press, 1998), 18.

2. Oral testimony before the National Bioethics Advisory Commission cited in Eliot Marshall, "Mammalian Cloning Debate Heats Up," *Science*, 275(1997), 1773.

3. Cf. Jeffrey Stout, *Ethics After Babel: The Languages of Morals and Their Discontents* (Boston: Beacon Press, 1988), 193-200.

the profound sense of anxiety provoked by recent scientific developments and to account for the relationship between the two.

Arguments against cloning human beings have been put forward on a number of grounds. There are concerns about the safety of cloning techniques, as well as issues related to the commodification of children. Some commentators have addressed threats to the integrity of family structures or have drawn attention to the unreasonable expectations that might be placed on those who are born as a result of cloning. Others have spoken of the implied arrogance and hubris in the attempt to reproduce oneself and/or gain such tight control over the future of human biology. While all of these concerns are, in my view, very real and merit careful ethical and theological reflection, none of them, alone or even taken together, quite accounts for the strength of the reaction that followed the announcement of the achievements of the Roslin team. Furthermore, relatively little of the reaction focused on the cloning of sheep, the breakthrough that had been achieved at Roslin. Instead, attention turned to the possibility of repeating the process using human beings. While that might be an entirely understandable focus of concern, it serves to draw attention away from the extraordinary technological power unleashed by the new technique, especially when placed in conjunction with other recent developments in the field of biotechnology.

What cloning by nuclear transfer allows is the cloning of an adult animal, one whose characteristics are known. Older, pre-Dolly technologies of mammalian cloning involved splitting the early embryo into individual cells, each of which is then allowed to develop into an adult organism. However, this technique is limited in the number of clones that can be produced. Mice can be split at the two-cell stage and cattle and sheep embryos at the eight-cell stage (although no one had ever recovered all eight possible offspring). By using the Roslin technique, a potentially unlimited number of clones can be produced.

Even more important are the implications of combining the new cloning with the increasing power of genetic manipulation, which allows us to move genes quite freely and with increasing precision between one genome and another, even between one species and another. Thus, the cloning work at Roslin was conceived as part of a wider program to create sheep that would produce milk with commercially viable quantities of human proteins that could be used in the treatment of disease. The steps to that end included the production of Tracy, a sheep that was not cloned but that contained the human gene for alpha-1-antitrypsin, an enzyme that is defective in patients with cystic fibrosis and emphysema. After Dolly came the sheep Polly, which was cloned, although using the older technique of embryo splitting. Polly was engineered to carry the human gene for factor IX, a protein that contributes to blood clotting and whose deficiency causes hemophilia. The final thread in this picture is the emerging science of genomics, which is seeking to map the position and function of the various genes in a variety of organisms including human beings. The impact of these three areas of scientific development, taken together, is potentially staggering.

> Transfer of genes from organism to organism, and the creation of quite new genes [genetic engineering], makes it possible in principle to build new organisms at will. Genomics provides the necessary data: knowledge of what genes to transfer—where to find them, and what they do. Cloning makes it possible in principle to apply all the immense power of genetic engineering and genomics to animals.[4]

What is remarkable about the early debate engendered by the cloning of Dolly is that the actual achievements of the Roslin team and their implications were largely passed over in favor of a discussion of human cloning, and this despite the fact that with few exceptions, there seemed to be a consensus among scientists in the field that the attempt to clone a human person was not a desirable project. In the rush to condemn hypothetical human cloning, it seems that many of the moral challenges presented by the actual achievements of the Roslin team were either distorted or disappeared from view altogether.

Why did this happen? Patrick Hopkins suggests that the popular reaction was largely a product of the way in which the story was handled in the media.[5] Yet as Hopkins himself admits, the press

---

4. Ian Wilmut, "The Importance of Being Dolly," in Ian Wilmut, Keith Campbell, and Colin Tudge, *The Second Creation: Dolly and the Age of Biological Control* (New York: Farrar, Straus and Giroux, 2000), 9.

5. Patrick D. Hopkins "Bad Copies: How Popular Media Represent Cloning as an Ethical Problem," *Hastings Center Report,* 28:2 (1998): 6-13

could not simply have created an anxiety that was not already present to some degree in the popular consciousness. Press reports capture the popular imagination most effectively when they reflect and articulate concerns that are already present. Timothy Renick suggests that the visceral reaction to the cloning of Dolly, and to the possibility of cloning a human being, lies in the challenge such a possibility offers to the most fundamental ways in which we organize and understand our world. Drawing on the work of Jeffrey Stout and Mary Douglas, Renick notes that cloning threatens to confuse the most basic of human relationships:

> The lines between mother and sister or father and son, for example, necessarily are blurred by somatic cell nuclear transfer cloning in a way they are not by in vitro fertilization, artificial insemination, or even cloning by embryo splitting. The unsettling fact is that the woman who seeks reproduction by nuclear transfer cloning is simultaneously the biological mother and genetic sister of her cloned offspring.[6]

It is this fundamental confusion of the categories through which we understand and shape the most basic of human relationships that is the source of the moral revulsion and outrage that are expressed in the cloning debate.

For Renick, recognizing the source of our discomfort is only the beginning of the debate, because the cosmological theories that underlie our most fundamental understandings of the world and our place in it come and go. Some of these theories are bound to cultural chauvinisms that fail to stand the test of time. Others seem more deeply rooted and enduring, perhaps even universal. However, two questions arise at this point. First, what theological resources might help us both to illuminate and to weigh such cosmological commitments? If, as Renick suggests, they have functioned in the background of the debates around human cloning they can only distort the debate by concealing the real nature of our concerns. How might theological analysis of such commit-

---

6. Timothy M. Renick, "A Cabbit in Sheep's Clothing: Exploring the Sources of our Moral Disquiet about Cloning," *Annual of the Society of Christian Ethics*, 18(1998): 267

ments ground them in a way that might be constructive? Second, how might such commitments function in the discussion, not of human cloning alone, but of the real technological powers that open before us as a result of the convergence of the biotechnologies that come together in the cloning of Dolly? In particular, what might our reaction be to so-called therapeutic cloning or to the use of cloning to make organs available for xenotransplantation?

Renick's approach is suggestive, although it does not really account for the difference between our reaction to cloning by embryo splitting and cloning using the Roslin technique. It might be more helpful to suggest that the real confusion is much more wide-ranging and therefore more unsettling from a variety of different perspectives than even Renick recognizes. We need to see this if we are to find theologically adequate ways of articulating the categories that are shaping our experience and that are challenged by the new biotechnologies. Perhaps the most urgent task, to which I turn next, is to consider how the recent advances in cloning technology, coupled with the other advances in biotechnology that I have referred to, cast doubt on the adequacy of arguments used to assess the moral status of the early embryo.

THE MORAL STATUS OF THE EMBRYO

The moral status of the early embryo is a subject of sharp debate. Some believe the early embryo is the moral equivalent of a fully developed human person. Although this approach might seem counterintuitive at first, it does have the advantage that it treats moral status as a given to be honored rather than as an achievement to be won. In principle this approach should be sensitive to the needs of the disadvantaged and vulnerable. In practice, it privileges a sort of vulnerability of being—a vulnerability linked to the undeveloped nature of the being of the embryo—and fails to pay sufficient attention to the concrete expressions of social, political, and economic vulnerability that disadvantage women and the poor. The approach also fails to take seriously the biological fact of enormous wastage as large numbers of conceptions either fail to implant in the uterus or end in miscarriage, sometimes before the pregnancy is even detected.

From the point of view of Ian Wilmut's work, however, there are further difficulties. The assertion of the moral inviolability of the early embryo is premised on two claims. First, it is asserted that at conception the egg and sperm come together to form a genetically unique being. Second, this new being has all of the genetic information and developmental potential, given the appropriate environment of the uterus, to develop into a human child. Thus the twin pegs of genetic uniqueness and potentiality for human life in all its richness form the basis for the ascription of full human moral dignity to the ball of cells that is the human embryo at the earliest stages of its development.

It is precisely these two characteristics, however, that are undermined by the techniques employed at Roslin. In the first place, no new genetic identity comes into being. Rather, a pre-existent genetic identity, the nuclear DNA from the ewe cloned to form Dolly, is placed into a cell that is undifferentiated and that can therefore be guided by the inserted DNA to form any tissue, or even a whole new sheep. There is no new genome formed, and it is not at all clear that nuclear transfer is either conceptually or morally the equivalent of conception. Second, the technique relies on new understandings of cell potentiality. Until recently, it was assumed that only during the first few cell divisions, before any differentiation had taken place, are cells capable of developing into all the different types of cells that form the human body. Once differentiation took place, cells are assigned to particular tasks and cease to be capable of forming different types of cells. However, with the discovery of stem cells it seems that this is not quite so clear.

Most tissues contain stem cells, cells that are capable of forming the various types of cell that make up muscle, skin, or a liver. We now know that some of those stem cells can be made to form a variety of types of cell other than those found in the tissues from which they are extracted. They do not have totipotency, the capacity to form any type of cell, but they do have pluripotency, the capacity to form many types of cells. Of particular interest in this regard are embryonic stem cells. These cells are taken from the embryo at a point when it is a ball of about a thousand cells differentiated into two broad regions, but before the primitive streak appears. Embryonic stem cells appear to be totipotent and have enormous potential for the development of cell lines for the treatment of degenerative diseases such as Parkinson's disease and for the growth of tissues for transplant. If they are truly totipotent, then theoretically it might become possible to develop them into whole human beings. Thus totipotency, the potentiality of a cell for full independent human life, a property previously assumed to belong only to the newly conceived embryo, may in fact appear later in the tissues of an embryo that has already begun differentiation. The point is that in the presence of the new biotechnologies neither of the characteristics used to express the moral status of the early embryo helps us to draw clear and morally helpful lines.

MORAL AMBIGUITY AND PUBLIC POLICY

The problems that I am pointing to can be illustrated by drawing attention to recent policy changes in Britain and the United States. In the latter, the National Institutes of Health (NIH) has issued new rules that will allow federally funded researchers to work on human embryonic stem cells, provided those cells were derived from embryos that were not produced by any agency or researcher receiving federal funding, and provided the embryos were not produced for the purposes of extracting cells.[7] The major likely source will be the surplus embryos that are produced by fertility clinics, embryos that would normally be destroyed if no longer needed. For those who believe that these embryos are human persons, their destruction is tantamount to murder, but this is not the official position of the majority of the mainstream churches. For them the early embryo has moral worth and should not be treated as a mere thing, but it is not yet a human person. It is a being with the capacity to become a human person. A similar sort of distinction might be seen in the current policies in Canada and the United Kingdom that allow research on embryos up to fourteen days, provided the embryos are not produced for the purposes of research. The fourteen-day limit is based on the time of the appearance of the primitive streak, the first sign of the development of the central nervous

7. http://www.nih.gov/news/stemcell/stemcellguidelines.htm and http://www.nih.gov/news/stemcell/stemfactsheet.htm

system. It is the central nervous system that will later play a crucial role in the coordination of the organism, in the experience of pain, and in the development of characteristics such as consciousness and the capacity for human thought and emotion.

For those churches that have relied on a developmental approach to the ascription of moral worth to the early embryo, it is hard to see what the objection to fetal cell research might consistently be, provided appropriate consents have been given. The production of the embryos, on this model, is for the purposes of implantation. More embryos are usually produced than can be implanted. If the early embryo is not yet a human person, does it really show more respect to the embryo to leave it frozen indefinitely rather than to destroy it, or to simply destroy it rather than to conduct research that will further our understanding of the proper development of embryos? If we can do these things, why can we not extract tissues from the embryo that will have significant therapeutic use? The situation is further complicated by the fact that it might not be necessary to destroy an embryo in order to extract stem cells. It is in principle possible to extract such cells from an embryo intended for implantation and then culture them. In such a case we would be dealing with tissues that had been obtained without "harm" to an embryo, but which, if they are truly totipotent, might in principle be cultured in such a way that they could possibly be developed into an implantable embryo. Would such cells be embryos or "potential" embryos? And on the basis of the sorts of arguments advanced above, what would their moral status be?

It is instructive to compare these proposed changes with recent proposals for change in the United Kingdom. The recently released Donaldson Report goes beyond the American initiative. One of the problems with the use of tissues produced from embryonic stem cells is that they may not be completely compatible with the immune system of the patient for whom they are intended. There are two alternative approaches that promise greater compatibility. One is to use stem cells taken from the patient's own tissues to replace damaged cells and perhaps to modify them modify them before replacing them. However, most stem cells are much less flexible than embryonic stem cells. A further alternative is to use cloning by nuclear transfer to produce an embryo from which stem cells will be extracted in order to produce the tissues or cell lines that are needed. The Donaldson Report sees this type of therapeutic cloning as unproblematic because it does not involve any uses of the early embryo other than those already allowed.[8] However, as the Church of Scotland's Science Religion and Technology Project points out, there is one significant difference. The proposed production of embryos for the sole purpose of being sources of spare body parts appears to involve far greater commodification of the embryo than current uses. Thus, although the Church of Scotland was willing to support limited use of embryos in research, it concluded that

> up to now, permitted research . . . still treats the embryo as an entity in itself, and is for the long-term benefit of other embryos. The proposed use of an embryo simply as a source of body cells is a very different notion both scientifically and ethically. It would reduce the embryo to a mere resource from which convenient parts are taken.[9]

I am certainly sympathetic with this approach, but the argument as presented is problematic because of ambiguities in the status given to the early embryo. On the one hand, there seems to be some concern to give the embryo a similar status to that of a human person. It is noted that some in the church do see the embryo as a human person and would permit no research that was not for the benefit of a particular embryo. The official position seems willing, however, to countenance research for the benefit of embryos in general. Already the embryo is treated as a means to the good of other embryos rather than as an end in itself. Further, it is not clear to me why allowing other embryos to benefit from such research, but not persons who are no longer embryos, shows more respect to the embryo or treats it with more dignity. Since the benefits of greater knowledge about embryos are always, in the final analysis, benefits to other persons, there seems to be some casuistic sleight of hand here.

---

8. http://www.doh.gov.uk/cegc/stemcellreport.htm.

9. Society, Religion and Technology Background Paper, "Kirk Questions Donaldson Report: Embryos Should Not Become Resources," Edinburgh, August 16, 2000; cf. Donald Bruce, Chapter 3, this volume, for further discussion.

At the very least we are dealing with an ambivalence that is clearly reflected in the report's defense of an unspecified "special status" for the embryo. The difficulty is that when we begin to speak of the embryo more concretely, as the entity that recent scientific advances show it to be, the distinctions by which we have sought to shape our behavior toward the embryo begin to appear less and less helpful and their application almost inevitably becomes more arbitrary. This does not mean that our former intuitions about the status of the embryo are wrong. But it does mean that they cannot offer us a clear-cut set of responses to the recent developments and promise of biotechnology. Further, it points to precisely the sort of ambiguity and dislocation of our experience that gives rise to anxiety and raises the temperature of moral debate.

MORAL GUIDEPOSTS FOR THE FUTURE

The question of the embryo's status is not the only place where we are unsure of ourselves. Consider how we answer the question, Why pursue genetics at all? The most clearly stated reason for the pursuit of the new biotechnologies is the amelioration of genetically linked illness and premature death. At the present time, it is estimated that susceptibility to more than four thousand diseases is genetically linked. In some cases, these diseases are severe, even catastrophic, as in the case of cystic fibrosis, muscular dystrophy, and Huntington's chorea.

Genetic illness sometimes is linked to the actions of complex groups of genes, each of which may have more than one function. In a few cases, genetic illness is linked to changes in one gene whose effects are quite predictable. It is this latter group of illnesses for which there is some hope that genetic therapy might prove effective. In principle, it would involve genetically modifying cells from the patient to replace the defective gene with one that works properly. This would be called somatic cell modification. It affects the somatic or body cells of the patient, but not the genes that are passed to offspring (germ line cells). The technologies of gene modification can in principle be used to modify an early embryo produced by in vitro fertilization, which could then be implanted. This would affect not only the baby born as a result of this technique but also all future generations and is thus called germ line therapy.

To date, the results of somatic cell genetic therapy are rather disappointing.[10] Still, there is a burgeoning literature on genetic therapy with what appears to be an emerging consensus that while somatic cell modification may hold some promise, germ line modification is too fraught with risk to be acceptable.[11] However, the possibility of any significant genetic modification raises sharply the question as to which genetic differences should be seen as anomalous, "abnormal," or as illnesses to be treated, and which genetic differences represent variations within the normal range. The documented use of growth hormone for children who are at the low end of the normal height range, although not a genetic therapy, is illustrative of the ease with which we can move between therapeutic intervention, which is designed to alleviate illness, and enhancement, which aims to improve on particular desirable characteristic.[12] The techniques that I am considering in this chapter—genomics, genetic engineering, and cloning—promise to increase greatly our power to intervene either to heal or to enhance.

Even if we limit genetic technology to healing, we must see how close genetics lies to eugenics. It is not surprising that groups representing people with disabilities have been made anxious by the energy that has been put into the development of the new genetic technologies. They fear a diminution of resources available to them as more money is put into programs to prevent genetic illness and fewer funds are available for treatment and resources for people with disabilities. They fear discrimination as our genetic power leads to an increasing preoccupation with defects and abnormalities and to the stigmatizing of those thought to possess genes for undesirable traits. Jeremy Rifkin suggests that we should all fear the expansion of the range of characteristics that are considered abnormalities and made appropriate objects of therapeutic intervention:

10. David L. Wheeler, "Few Successes in Gene Therapy," *Chronicle of Higher Education*, July 14, 1995, A8.

11. Cf. Audrey Chapman's article in this volume.

12. Jeremy Rifkin, *The Biotech Century: Harnessing the Gene and Remaking the World* (New York: Penguin, 1998), 141-42. See also Mary Terrell White, "Making Responsible Decisions: An Interpretive Ethic for Genetic Decisionmaking," *Hastings Center Report*, 29:1(1999): 14-21

"Genetic engineering technologies are, by their very nature, eugenics tools."[13] While some may find his warnings lacking in nuance, the difficulties of adequately distinguishing between normal and abnormal, therapeutic and eugenic, are striking. The serious challenge this raises to central explanatory categories, which in the past have functioned to assist decision making in this area, is surely a partial explanation of the strength of reaction, particularly within some communities, to the new technologies. This brings us again to Renick's suggestion about the sources of our moral disquiet around cloning by suggesting that the group of biotechnologies that surround the achievements of the Roslin team, and enhance the potential impact of cloning, all contribute to an undermining of the explanatory models by which we have shaped our reaction to a number of ethical quandaries. I want now to suggest that this challenge reaches into the very heart of our sense of uniqueness, not simply in our relationship to each other, but in our relationship to the surrounding world.

It is an old and commonplace observation for developmental biologists that, "embryogeny mirrors phylogeny." In other words, the development of the embryo shows us something of our biological roots: our evolution from the ancestors we share with other species. Human beings do not *have* an environment, they *are part of* the environment. Theologically, this should not be particularly startling. The primary theological divide has always been between the creator and the creation, with human beings firmly on the side of creation, as part of the natural world. However, a great deal of ethical reflection has derived important insights from the distinctions between human beings and the rest of nature. The lengthy debates about the ascription of rights, our primary moral language, have tended to assume that human beings have certain qualities, not shared by the rest of the created world, which make them the bearers of rights. We are used to being able to manipulate the natural world to produce goods for the betterment of the human condition, and what the current biotechnologies do is to offer the promise (or threat) of a similar control over the life and development of human beings.

---

13. Jeremy Rifkin, *Biotech Century*, 116, cf. 128.

Does this appeal to us because of hubris? Does it draw us because we subscribe to what Richard Lewontin has called the myth of genetic determinism?[14] There is little doubt that in popular culture, genetic determinism is a powerful myth at present, and as our potential to shape our genetic inheritance increases, it is a myth that serves to undercut our sense of moral uniqueness. The new technologies are, after all, about our ability to objectify and manipulate our own genetic material as so much stuff. At the same time, there is a growing awareness of the strong resemblances between our DNA and that of other primates. Add to these two elements the belief, supported by a triumphalist biotechnology industry, that what we are is "all in the genes," and there is the basis for a vigorous challenge of any claim to human uniqueness. Once again, a category by which we have ordered experience and shaped our moral comportment is challenged. Once again, we see grounds for the sort of moral dissonance that comes when our fundamental categories are challenged.

Claims of repugnance in the absence of the sort of discursive moral reasons that are normally offered in public policy discourse do not lead to a stable position. But as Jeffrey Stout and others have suggested, such claims, far from being mere exercises in arbitrariness, may reflect a fundamental challenge to the categories by which our culture organizes its experience of nature and of the way things ought to be. This challenge should neither be accepted uncritically nor be dismissed by moral/logical reductive strategies. It is too easy to imply that what cannot be accounted for by existing ethical theories, or argumentative strategies, is simply irrational. A more adequate response to claims of repugnance in response to the possibility of human cloning will not seek simply to dismiss the reaction, but to explain it as Renick and others have suggested. Biotechnology mounts a broad challenge to our ordinary ways of looking at ourselves in nature. The work at Roslin, no less than that of Copernicus or Einstein, requires that we rearticulate the "cosmological categories" by which we shape our relationships to each other and to the world around us. That is a properly theological task, one that I have only begun.

---

14. Richard C. Lewontin, *Biology as Ideology: The Doctrine of DNA* (Concord, Ont.: Anansi Press, 1991).

5

Religious Perspective on
Human Germ Line Modifications

Audrey R. Chapman

Looking even further into the future at the question of human germ line modification (gene modifications that are inheritable), Audrey Chapman explores the religious and moral questions that lie ahead. Assume for the moment that someday we will have the technology to modify the genes that we pass to our offspring. What good may come from this power, and what evil? How can the risks and the benefits be distributed justly? How can we human beings have the foresight to use a technology that will affect a thousand generations to come? Drawing upon a recent study, Chapman offers a detailed analysis of the ethics of one of the twenty-first century's most awe-inspiring technologies.

During its first ten years of existence, the field of gene therapy was rightly criticized for promising too much and delivering too little. Now, after nearly a decade of unsuccessful gene therapy trials, scientists are beginning to report encouraging results. In 2000, scientists reported success with gene therapy for treating two genetic diseases, inherited severe combined immunodeficiency (SCID) and hemophilia, as well as progress in growing new blood vessels to treat cardiovascular disease and developing gene-based vaccines for treating some types of cancer.[1] Breakthroughs like these, together with the completion of the Human Genome Project, are conferring upon medicine the ability to undertake gene therapies involving various techniques as

---

1. W. French Anderson, "The Best of Times, the Worst of Times," *Science* 288 (28 April 2000): 627-629.

possible remedies for diseases caused by inherited genetic defects, particularly for diseases caused by abnormalities in single genes.

Members of religious communities should, and no doubt will, welcome these developments. But it is also important to recognize that these successes raise new ethical and theological questions about the next steps in the genetic revolution. To date, most research and clinical resources have been invested in somatic cell gene therapy, which attempts to treat a disease by adding or altering a specific gene in the cells of the patient receiving treatment. Recent advances in research in animals are now raising the possibility that scientists will have the technical capacity at some point in the future to modify genes that are transmitted to future generations. Germ or reproductive cells are the body cells that develop into the egg or sperm of a developing organism and convey its heritable characteristics to offspring. The germ line includes gametes, sperm and egg cells, as well as the cells from which they are derived. Future efforts to treat disease by altering the genes that are passed to future generations is usually referred to as "germ line gene therapy." But with the greater knowledge of genetics that makes gene therapy possible, it will also become possible to contemplate going beyond genetic interventions to treat health problems and to consider applications to enhance or improve normal human characteristics, such as height or intelligence.

Germ line gene therapy and even germ line enhancement have their advocates. These advocates generally cite several reasons for developing and applying germ line technologies. In theory, modifying the genes that are transmitted to future generations offers potential advantages over somatic cell gene therapy. Inheritable genetic interventions provide the possibility of economically eliminating the inheritance of some genetically based diseases rather than repeating somatic therapy generation after generation. Because germ line intervention would be performed at the earliest stage of human development, it offers the potential for preventing irreversible damage that in some cases occurs as early as the first weeks of a pregnancy. For these diseases, somatic cell therapy would be too late. Some scientists and ethicists argue that germ line intervention is medically necessary to prevent genetic disorders that cannot be identified through screening and embryo selection procedures. Others anticipate that the ability to correct genetic disorders will eliminate the need for therapeutic abortions. Over a long period of time, germ line gene transfers could decrease the incidence of certain inherited diseases that currently cause great suffering. These arguments are meant to support the position that we should develop this technology because it is moral to do so because good patient care requires it. But it should also be noted that some recent literature seems to celebrate the technological imperative, that is, the sense that we will and should apply any technologies that are developed whatever their ethical consequences or social costs.[2]

Despite the arguments put forward by the advocates of germ line modifications, it should be clear that these technologies raise profound ethical, theological, and policy issues that need to be thoroughly discussed and evaluated, preferably well before these technologies are developed. Efforts to modify the genes that are transmitted to future generations entail much more than a medical revolution because they offer us the power to mold ourselves in a variety of novel ways. These techniques could give us extraordinary control of biological properties and personality traits that are fundamental to our humanness. Even if we have the technical ability to proceed, we would need to determine whether we have the wisdom, ethical commitment, and public policies necessary to apply these technologies in a manner that is equitable, just, and respectful of human dignity.

From the beginnings of the genetic revolution, religious communities and thinkers have affirmed the promise of genetic technologies to treat and prevent disease while also demonstrating uneasiness or anxiety about the implications of altering the genetic basis of life. Virtually all religious communities and thinkers have supported somatic gene intervention for therapeutic purposes, provided its safety is demonstrated. As might be anticipated, germ line alterations that

---

2. In March 1998, a symposium titled "Engineering the Human Germline" was held at UCLA. A publication was issued based on the symposium presentations. See Gregory Stock and John Campbell, editors, *Engineering the Human Germline: An Exploration of the Science and Ethics of Altering the Genes We Pass to Our Children* (Oxford and New York: Oxford University Press, 2000). Lee Silver, a biologist at Princeton University, has been a leading voice supporting human germ line intervention. See his book *Remaking Eden: How Genetic Engineering and Cloning Will Transform the American Family* (New York: Avon Books, 1998).

will affect the genetic inheritance of future generations have elicited greater reservations. Positions of religious bodies on the appropriateness of germ line therapy range from a studied and intentional silence in the policy statement of the National Council of Churches[3] to various documents that have articulated significant reservations about this technology. Perhaps the strongest example of this latter category is a 1992 Methodist statement: "Because its long-term effects are uncertain, we oppose therapy that results in changes that can be passed to offspring."[4] Nevertheless, most religious bodies that have positions on the topic express caution rather than categorical rejection and emphasize the need for ethical reflection to develop guidelines before proceeding.[5] Even various Catholic agencies and thinkers have stated that germ line intervention would not necessarily be theologically prohibited, provided the technology met certain conditions: it did not diminish or alter human nature, the technology were to be made safe, and it became possible for modifications to be made on ova or sperm so as to avoid the use of in vitro fertilization.[6]

A recently completed study of the prospects for and implications of developing human germ line modification sponsored by the American Association for the Advancement of Science (AAAS), which I coauthored, identifies a series of ethical issues that the development and application of this technology would raise.[7] Many of the scientific and ethical issues the report explores will be of particular concern to the religious community.

---

3. National Council of Churches of Christ in the U.S.A., "Genetic Science for Human Benefit," New York, Office of Research and Evaluation, adopted by the Governing Board, May 22, 1986.

4. United Methodist Church, *Book of Discipline of the United Methodist Church* (Nashville: United Methodist Publishing House, 1992), 97-98.

5. See, for example, World Council of Churches, *Biotechnology: Its Challenge to the Churches and the World* (Geneva: WCC, 1989), 14.

6. Working Party of the Catholic Bishops Joint Committee, *Genetic Intervention on Human Subjects* (London: Catholic Bishops Joint Committee, 1996), 31; *Human Genetics: Ethical Issues in Genetic Testing, Counseling, and Therapy* (St. Louis: Catholic Health Association of the United States, 1990), 20-22.

7. Mark S. Frankel and Audrey R. Chapman, *Intergenerational Genetic Modifications: A Working Group Report* (Washington, D.C.: American Association for the Advancement of Science, 2000).

SAFETY CONSIDERATIONS

From the very beginning of the genetic revolution the religious community has worried about safety considerations related to these technologies. Many religious thinkers evince what might be described as a presumption of caution. That is, they place greater priority on anticipating and preventing potential problems than on favoring genetic developments because they may bring future benefits to some persons. Because germ line interventions would be transmitted to the progeny of the person treated, there is a particular need for compelling scientific evidence that these procedures are safe, effective, and stable across generations before proceeding with human trials.

The AAAS report advocates for stringent criteria to ascertain that germ line technologies meet safety standards. There needs to be evidence that the procedures do not cause unacceptable deleterious short-term or long-term consequences either for the treated individual or succeeding generations of offspring. To meet this standard, an altered embryo would have to be able to transit all human developments without mishaps due to the artificially induced intervention.

However, not only is it not yet possible to meet these standards, it is unlikely that we will be able to do so for the foreseeable future. The AAAS report concludes that current somatic technologies, which add genetic material to compensate for mutations rather than correcting a defective gene in an attempt to restore cell function, are not appropriate for germ line gene transfers. These somatic methods have a number of serious technical problems, such as the inability to deliver corrective genes to the right place in the genome. Genes that are expressed in the wrong tissues, or wrong developmental stage, or at the wrong levels may have deleterious effects. Modifying the germ line while leaving the defective gene in place also raises the possibility that the disease might reappear in future generations. Because gene addition techniques introduce viruses and other matter to cells, they also add to the risk of unintended harms. Like human somatic therapy, efforts to modify the germ line in animals have been inefficient and unpredictable.

How much risk should we be willing to assume to undertake germ line modifications? No new biomedical technology is ever completely safe. The subjects for somatic gene trials have had few other treatment options, but the AAAS report concluded that there were relatively few situations where there were no alternatives to germ line therapy. It is very important to set standards of safety and efficacy for human germ line intervention well before the technology is developed. Otherwise, some scientists may be tempted to rush to human trials. This is an ethical as well as a scientific issue. Mistakes in animals can be discarded. This approach is not acceptable for humans.

One of the complications in determining safety is that some risks from the interventions may remain latent and not manifest themselves for generations. Germ line modifications require multigenerational data over sixty to eighty years on which to make conclusive determinations of safety and efficacy. While additional experience with somatic cell gene therapy will help clarify some of the risks from genetically engineering human cells, it will not be able to show multigenerational effects. Animal research, particularly trials with higher primates, will be a valuable source of data, but it will not be conclusive for assessing the effects on human subjects. Many members of the AAAS working group, including several of the scientists, therefore questioned whether we will ever have enough confidence in the safety of germ line interventions to proceed to clinical use.

INEQUALITIES IN ACCESS

Christianity has a commitment to social and economic justice that derives from the belief that the benefits of creation, including those that come in part from human effort, are meant to be widely shared. This makes many within the religious community particularly sensitive to the issue of equity in access to new biomedical technologies. Unless there are major changes in the health care system in the United States, there will likely be a fundamental lack of equity in access to germ line therapies.[8] This reflects a number of factors: the

---

8. See, for example, Audrey R. Chapman, "Justice Implications of Germ Line Modifications, " in Audrey R. Chapman and Mark S. Frankel, editors, *Human Genetic Modifications Across Generations: Assessing Scientific, Ethical, Religious, and Policy Issues (forthcoming)*.

absence of universal health insurance, patterns of inequalities in access to health care, a projected scarcity in the availability of genetic services relative to demand, and the role of market forces in the development of such genetic interventions. Current limitations on access to health care for minorities, who are far more likely to be uninsured as compared to whites, are likely to operate with respect to genetic services as well. At least initially, access will undoubtedly also be limited by the need for considerable knowledge and sophistication to take advantage of such a complex technology.

For all of these reasons, the AAAS report concludes that germ line technologies most likely will be available only to those with expensive private insurance or sufficient wealth to purchase these services. At a minimum, most private insurers may be inclined to delay agreeing to reimburse policyholders for these genetic services until their efficacy and safety are clearly demonstrated. Another likely impediment to accessibility is the refusal of most health insurers to pay for high-technology reproductive services like in vitro fertilization. Additionally, health insurance policies rarely cover anything considered to be nontherapeutic, such as cosmetic surgery. This would of course apply to enhancement modifications. While it remains to be seen how costly these techniques will be, their development by the private sector on a for-profit basis means that they will likely be beyond the means of many citizens, making them available only to a narrow, wealthy segment of society.

JUSTICE IMPLICATIONS

Many, perhaps most, new technologies tend to benefit some groups and disadvantage others. Religious ethicists writing on genetics tend to be very sensitive to these justice considerations. Also, the understanding of justice and its requirements is generally broader among religious thinkers. When religious ethicists deal with justice issues they often emphasize the need for preferential access for the disadvantaged. As noted above, the reverse is likely to occur.

To make techniques for germ line intervention available in a system based on the ability to pay would be very problematic, even if employed only on a small scale. It would add inherited advantages to all the advantages of nurture and education already enjoyed by the affluent, and constitute one more brick in the wall dividing "haves" from "have-nots." To mitigate this impact, the AAAS working group recommended that reform of the health-care system to make access to genetic services available on a more equitable basis was an important ethical prerequisite of going forward with germ line therapies. Some members of the working group also held the view that a society in which one-sixth of the members do not have health insurance and reliable access to basic health services should not be making investments in such expensive genetic innovations. Other members argued that it is pointless to talk about any kind of just distribution of genetic technologies unless and until all persons everywhere have access to adequate nutrition, potable water, sanitation, and basic vaccinations for children. Still others took issue with this perspective, responding that the world is full of inequalities of health care, but we do not therefore restrict research and use of promising medical technologies.

REINFORCE EXISTING DISCRIMINATION

The AAAS working group was concerned that as long as Americans continued to discriminate unfairly on the basis of physical appearance, ancestry, or abilities, the introduction of germ line modifications would pose some risk of exacerbating social prejudices. This is particularly a problem in a country like the United States, which has a long and disturbing history of drawing sharp distinctions among citizens on the basis of race and ethnicity and where many persons harbor beliefs in biological determinism. Germ line technologies may have the inadvertent effect of particularly increasing discrimination against persons with disabilities. Given the expense of caring for children born with genetic defects, it is also plausible that some insurance companies will pressure known carriers of genetic mutations to use germ line modification to preclude the birth of a child with a genetic disease.

CHALLENGES TO EQUALITY

As early as 1982 the President's Commission for the Study of Ethical Problems in Medicine and Biomedical and Behavioral Research raised the concern that human germ line therapy could create enormous social injustices.[9] Subsequently, other analysts have warned that the genetic revolution will pose unprecedented challenges to equal opportunity, particularly in a society with unequal access to health care, such as ours.[10] Ethicists have expressed concern that the technology will be able to enhance offspring in socially desirable and competitive ways, thereby further privileging the wealthy and powerful by securing the position of their offspring against competition.[11]

The AAAS working group anticipated that the availability of germ line modifications could very well significantly magnify inequalities already rooted in American culture. Germ line changes would have a cumulative impact; the advantages and enhancements of one generation would be passed on to their progeny. Many members of the working group were very concerned that unequal access to these technologies would mean that those persons who can already provide the best "environments" for their children would also be able to purchase the best "natures." Thus, those who had preferential access to life's material goods would be able to purchase genetic improvements for their children and their children's descendants, and therefore become doubly advantaged. How much of an advantage this would confer and thereby contribute to inequality would depend, of course, on the types of modifications that will become possible.

RELATIONSHIP BETWEEN PARENTS AND CHILDREN

Religious traditions tend to emphasize the relational dimensions of human life. A religious centering, by its very nature, offers a vision

---

9. President's Commission for the Study of Ethical Problems in Medicine and Biomedical and Behavioral Research, *Splicing Life: The Social and Ethical Issues of Genetic Engineering with Human Beings* (Washington, D.C.: U.S. Government Printing Office, 1982), 67.

10. Thomas H. Murray, "Introduction: The Human Genome Project and Access to Health Care," in Thomas H. Murray, Mark A. Rothstein, and Robert F. Murray Jr., *The Human Genome Project and the Future of Health Care*, (Bloomington, Ind.: Indiana University Press, 1996), ix.

11. A recent statement dealing with this issue is the "Resolution Opposing Experimental Research for and the Act of Genetic Engineering," voted by the Thirty-eighth Annual Conference Session of the United Methodist Youth Fellowship of the North Carolina Conference of the United Methodist Church, July 23, 1999.

in which persons are responsible beyond their own self-interest to the ultimate source of grounding of their lives and beings. That religious ethicists tend to go beyond an individualist perspective may also reflect their own sense of connectedness to a community, a tradition, and ultimately the divine. Religious thinkers often have a social conception of personhood. This view of the world sees value in structures and relationships such as family.

Thus, some religious thinkers are concerned that too much technological intervention in the genetic inheritance of offspring will undermine the value and meaning of the parent-child relationship. Simply put, the intrusion of technology, even if very well intended, could result in children being treated as artifacts. Rather than accepting any child born to them, parents would assume the role of designers determining the genetic code of their offspring. If competitive parents keen for "success" for their offspring were to create designer babies at will and whim, this would undermine our ethical ideal of unconditional acceptance of children, no matter what their abilities and traits. This would constitute a further corruption of parenting and of human relationships in general.

Some ethicists and religious thinkers also fear that human germ line manipulation would accelerate tendencies to commodify children and evaluate them according to standards of quality control.[12] In the existing market-based system of financing health care and related research, the patient is thought of in economic terms as consumer and the health-care provider as a seller of services on the open market. In circumstances in which the pull of commerce is powerful, it will be difficult to erect barriers to prevent the wholesale treatment of genetic intervention as a commodity in the marketplace. Obviously, germ line modification will not constitute the source of the attitudes that make science and medicine just one more form of concentrated social power or turn parenting into an exercise of power over offspring for the sake of the satisfaction of

---

12. See, for example, Cynthia Cohen, "Creating Tomorrow's Children: The Right to Reproduce and Oversight Germ Line Interventions," and Sondra Wheeler, "Parental Liberty and the Right of Access to Germ Line Intervention," in Frankel and Chapman, *Human Genetic Modifications Across Generations: Assessing Scientific, Ethical, Religious, and Policy Issues* (forthcoming).

parental desires. But it might well accelerate such attitudes by providing parents with a powerful tool.

THERAPY VERSUS ENHANCEMENT

Like somatic cell interventions, germ line technologies offer the possibility of undertaking genetic alterations intended to improve what are already "normal" genes. This procedure is termed genetic enhancement. Many in the religious community distinguish between, on the one hand, the acceptability of somatic cell therapy, and possible germ line interventions as well, for therapeutic purposes, and their inappropriateness for enhancing human traits, on the other.

One of the reasons why a distinction is made between therapeutic and enhancement germ line intervention is the fear that the ability to discard unwanted traits and improve wanted characteristics would lead to a form of eugenics. First used by Francis Galton in 1883, eugenics, meaning "good birth," became a movement in the early part of the twentieth century with the goal of weeding out what proponents believed were the "bad" traits of society and promoting "good" ones. When translated into state policy, eugenics can lead to serious abuses, as it did under the Nazis.[13] Contrary to the future projected in Aldous Huxley's 1932 novel *Brave New World,* there seems to be little likelihood of germ line technologies being used for state-sponsored compulsory eugenic programs. However, the emergence of a market-based "soft" eugenics stemming from parental use of germ line modifications to improve their children's genomes is a real possibility.[14]

Members of the AAAS working group, while provisionally willing to consider germ line intervention for therapeutic purposes at some

---

13. Roger Lincoln Shinn, *The New Genetics: Challenges for Science, Faith and Politics* (Wakefield, R.I., and London: Moyer Bell, 1996), 140; Arthur J. Dyck, "Eugenics in Historical and Ethical Perspectives," in John F. Kilner, Rebecca D. Pentz, and Frank E. Young, editors, *Genetic Ethics: Do the Ends Justify the Genes?* (Grand Rapids, Mich.: William B. Eerdmans, 1997), 25-32.

14. For a distinction between hard and soft eugenics, see Shinn, *The New Genetics,* 140.

point in the future provided the technology could meet stringent safety standards, had fundamental misgivings about undertaking genetic interventions to enhance traits of future generations. The dilemma, however, is that it may not be possible to draw a line between the acceptability of germ line intervention for therapeutic purposes and its inappropriateness for purposes of enhancement. The technology for therapy and enhancement procedures is fundamentally the same. Thus, developing the applications to correct defective genes is likely to promote creeping enhancement applications. For example, the ability to correct the genes responsible for Alzheimer's disease would mean that it might be possible to enhance intelligence as well. Also, given the larger size of the potential market for enhancement applications, biotechnology and pharmaceutical corporations are likely to invest heavily in and to promote such uses.

In theory, genetic enhancement could be accomplished through either somatic or germ line intervention. Whether or not germ line intervention will set us down a slippery slope toward enhancements, the desire to undertake enhancements will most likely favor germ line modification over somatic technology. Genetic enhancements are likely to require altering several genes that work in concert with each other. The genetic intervention is likely to be more effective when conducted early in the development of the embryo or on the fetus in utero. In many, perhaps most instances, such early intervention would result in alteration of the germ line whether or not it was intended.[15] The considerable expense involved might incline parents to try to get the most for their investment, again favoring the germ line option. Medical centers offering somatic gene therapies are also less likely than in vitro fertilization clinics to promote germ line enhancements and to encourage prospective parents to maximize their investment in reproductive services.[16]

---

15. Maxwell J. Mehlman and Jeffrey R. Botkin, *Access to the Genome: The Challenge to Equality* (Washington, D.C.: Georgetown University Press, 1998), 34.

16. See Mark S. Frankel and Michele S. Garfinkel, "To Market, To Market: The Effects of Commerce on Germ Line Intervention," in Frankel and Chapman, *Human Genetic Modifications Across Generations: Assessing Scientific, Ethical, Religious, and Policy Issues* (forthcoming)

CONCLUSION

Typically, our society proceeds in a "reactionary mode," scrambling to match our values and policies with scientific developments. The furor over the possibility of cloning human beings through the application of the somatic cell nuclear transfer technology used to clone the lamb Dolly underscores the importance of conducting a serious examination of the scientific, ethical, religious, and policy implications of new technologies in advance of scientific breakthroughs. It is far more difficult to have an informed and unemotional public discussion after a scientific discovery is announced than before it becomes a reality.

With any scientific advance that raises profound issues related to the possibilities of modifying our genetic futures, it is important, indeed essential, that the religious community play a role in shaping the discussion and decision making. To do so requires considerable knowledge of the science. For the religious community to proceed beyond generalities and to offer clear guidelines will also necessitate the development of a scientifically based prescriptive ethics infused with religious insight and values. Those in the religious community who are concerned about our genetic futures need to begin work now.

6

A Case against Cloning

Gilbert Meilaender

Returning now to the question of reproductive human cloning,
Gilbert Meilaender invites us to ask what we will lose if we turn to
cloning. What is the true cost of cloning that we will impose upon
our own humanity, our relationships as parents and children, and
the dignity of each human life? Against those who think that
cloning is unproblematic and acceptable as soon as it is safe,
Meilaender argues that it matters very much how we come into
existence and how we extend life to the next generation. In seeking
to replicate ourselves, will we only succeed in destroying ourselves?

I want to try to make the case against human cloning and to do
that, at least in part, in specifically Christian terms. Because that is
my task, however, I think I need to pause here at the outset to say
something about how the task shapes what I will do. For example,
there is more to be said about and against cloning than I will say,
so I will not address important questions about the cloning of animals or transgenic animals. I will focus on cloning that is intended to result in the live birth of a human being, not the cloning of
embryos for research purposes that would then be discarded.

These matters that I do not take up are important issues, and
they are, in some respects the chief focus of research interests just
now. They raise for us questions about the relation between human
beings and other animals and whether they are there simply for our
use. Also among these other matters are questions about the status
of human embryos and whether they are there simply for our use.
But I am going to push toward the larger sort of question that gal-
vanized public interest back in February of 1997, when news of the

cloning of Dolly first came to public attention. I will be thinking about attempts to gestate and give birth to a clone who replicates the genetic structure of an existing person.

Moreover, at least in part, certainly in the last part of what I have to say, I write in specifically theological terms, not just the standard language of bioethics or public policy. I do not think of mine, however, as the voice of a particular interest group, in this case the Christian one, weighing in with its interests in our public deliberations. On the contrary, this theological language seeks to uncover what is universal and human. It begins epistemologically from a particular place, but it opens up ontologically in a vision of the human.

These, then, are the boundaries of what I will be doing and the terms in which I approach the subject. I will be arguing that in trying to soar above natural human parenthood we may actually fall into a technological alienation of our humanity. In order to try to make this case, I want to look briefly at five reasons for concern about human cloning, using them to try to articulate a fundamental uneasiness about cloning that is, I think, fairly widespread.

The first problem, the ethics of experimentation, is the most straightforward. Remember that it took the Scottish researchers who produced Dolly 277 attempts, 277 transfers of adult nuclei into enucleated sheep eggs, to get 29 cloned embryos to implant in wombs. From those 29, they achieved the live birth of one lamb.

No doubt techniques will gradually improve, as will success rates. But they will improve only through experiments that, in the nature of the case, often fail. The success rate will not be high at first. Nor, by the way, has it been particularly high in reports of research cloning mice that have come out since the Dolly story. This means that there would be many failed experiments in the early stages of attempts to clone human beings.

Such attempts to clone a human being would be an experiment upon the child-to-be, who cannot consent to participate in such research. We cannot say what harms, mishaps, or deformities are possible. We can say pretty confidently that there would be many failed attempts involving subjects who cannot consent. This is exactly the sort of thing that violates generally accepted canons of research.

Now, of course, one might observe that these unconsenting subjects would, at first, be early embryos, and perhaps we could discard misfits at an early stage. How satisfying can that be, though, to avoid our mistakes by throwing them away? We know, of course, that the status of the early embryo is a subject of great debate, as the abortion controversy continues to make clear. But whatever precise view we take of the status of the early embryo, even those who recommend and approve of embryo research generally have used language of the following sort: They will say that the embryo should be treated with "profound respect." It is not clear to me how 276 botched attempts could constitute profound respect.

More generally, if we really want to take the language of autonomy seriously, we cannot think only about the autonomy of those people who desire to produce clones. We have to think also about the autonomy of those who would be produced through cloning. A willingness to forge ahead here with attempts at cloning would be a case of the strong happily using the weak for their own purposes. This realization ought to leave a bad taste in our mouths.

Having made this initial point about the morality of experimentation, I turn now to four other considerations, all of which are interconnected. All have to do, we might say, with the relation between the generations.

First, we need to think about the meaning of sexual reproduction. Leon Kass, a well-known scholar, has been especially effective in raising this question, and here I rely on some observations he has made. We find asexual reproduction only in the lowest forms of life (bacteria, algae, fungi, some lower invertebrates). There is a reason for this. It is, in fact, hard to imagine human life without sexual reproduction. Sexuality brings with it a certain kind of relationship to the world. It leads us to look out at the world in search of an "other" who complements us, who is both like us and different from us. With that "other" person we pursue a goal that transcends our individual existences, the generation of offspring. This is not just a rational or willed undertaking. It engages us wholly and entirely as bodily beings.

Thus, in our sexuality is the germ of our sociality. It draws us beyond ourselves and beyond even our most immediate kin. So sexuality is not a self-replicating or self-preserving activity. We look away from ourselves to another and together we give rise to the next generation, who will take our place. This is quite a different thing from cloning oneself. In sexual reproduction, unlike cloning, we look away from ourselves and we consent to our own mortality. That is part of what it means to be human, and it has its biological ground in our sexuality. This directs us to think about the identity of the clone. Here language almost fails us. How shall we describe the relation of the generations here? The clone will be twin to the person who is . . . what? His "father"? Or her "mother"? So are they siblings? Or parent and child? Genetics suggests one answer and age another.

Even though genes are not destiny, we lose something very important here, namely, the sense that this person's identity has not yet been lived. Indeed, it is clear that part of the reason we might be tempted to clone is that we think we know what we are getting. I suspect that many more people might want to have a clone than to be one, and that may have something to do with this matter of identity. Identity that is not mere replication has moral significance. In sexual reproduction, our children begin with a kind of genetic independence of us, their parents. They replicate neither their father nor their mother. This is a reminder of the independence that we must eventually grant to them and for which it is our duty to prepare them. They are different from us, not just the continuation of our projects or our way of being in the world. They are a gift entrusted to us. It is not clear that we could or would think about a clone in quite the same way.

Related to this question of identity is the slightly different question of control. In conceiving a child sexually, a man and woman are saying yes to the next generation. They are affirming that child, however he or she turns out. They are confessing the limits of their and our control. They are confessing, if they think about it seriously, that the child is not simply "their" child. The child does not exist simply for their happiness or fulfillment. To be sure, we have already forgotten this all too often. Attempts at conceiving children via in vitro fertilization can today involve preimplantation genetic diagnosis in which we decide whether to implant an embryo, accepting some, rejecting others. Prenatal diagnosis often followed by abortion if any defects are present is also less than an unqualified acceptance of the child. Even for children born in the natural manner, parents today are sometimes—perhaps often—all too eager to live vicariously through their children.

Cloning would give a new seal of approval to this tendency of ours to be despotic, to make children after our own image and in accord with our will. It would surely legitimize in principle the enterprise of designing children to suit our aims and purposes. By contrast, the sexual act, properly understood, confesses the limits of our control precisely when it is most creative. We find this point made in a poem by Galway Kinnell titled, "After Making Love We Hear Footsteps":

For I can snore like a bullhorn
or play loud music
or sit up talking with any reasonably sober Irishman
and Fergus will only sink deeper
into his dreamless sleep, which goes by all in one flash,
but let there be that heavy breathing
or a stifled come-cry anywhere in the house
and he will wrench himself awake
and make for it on the run as now, we lie together,
after making love, quiet, touching along the length of our bodies,
familiar touch of the long-married,
and he appears in his baseball pajamas, it happens,
the neck opening so small
he has to screw them on, which one day may make him wonder
about the mental capacity of baseball players
and flops down between us and hugs us and snuggles himself
    to sleep,
his face gleaming with satisfaction at being this very child.

In the half darkness we look at each other
And smile
And touch arms across his little, startlingly muscled body
this one whom habit of memory propels to the ground of his
    making,
Sleeper only the mortal sounds can sing awake,
This blessing love gives again into our arms.[1]

Think with me about that image. Why is the child "a blessing love gives again into our arms"? To understand this idea, we have to think a little about what lovemaking means. The act of love is not

---

1. Galway Kinnell, *Mortal Acts, Mortal Words* (Boston: Houghton Mifflin, 1980), 5.

simply a rational, willed undertaking. Of course, a man and a woman might decide to make love. They might choose to do it for certain reasons, for instance, to try to have a child. That is fine. But in the act itself, it is passion, not reason or will, that is central. We talk about lovers experiencing ecstasy, a word that means "to go out of oneself." You give yourself. You're not in control. You're setting aside your projects. Even if you want a child. Even if you're doing it just now because you want a child. The act itself requires that we let go of those plans and projects, that we let go and give ourselves.

So, if in the act itself we have no projects or purposes, suppose a child results. Then that child is not a product whom we've purposively created. That child is "a blessing love gives again into our arms," not one whom we control. Love giving is life giving, not because we so willed it, but because the Creator so blesses it. All that moral meaning is lost, and lost definitively, when we turn to cloning.

Finally, let me press this issue just a bit further to concerns about equal dignity. There is a kind of metaphysical underpinning to the understanding of the relation of parents and children that I developed in my previous point. If I develop this underpinning just a little, we can see why it has something to do with the equal dignity of all human beings, especially of parents and children.

Children conceived sexually are "begotten, not made." When a man and a woman beget a child, that child is formed out of what they are. What we beget is like ourselves, equal to us in dignity and not at our disposal. But what we *make* is not just like ourselves; it is the product of our free decision, and its destiny is ours to determine. So in cloning we give existence to a child not out of what we are, but solely through rational will and choice out of what we intend and design. This child is a product. We determine its destiny, and it is very hard, therefore, to think of it simply as equal to us in dignity.

That, I think, is the most fundamental issue of all. How we come into being is not a trivial matter. It is central to who we are. The phrase "begotten, not made" comes of course from the Nicene Creed, one of the two most important Christian creeds, dating from the fourth century.[2] It is language used to describe Jesus as the Son

---

2. Cf. Oliver O'Donovan, *Begotten or Made?* (Oxford: Clarendon Press, 1984).

of the Father. From eternity the Son is "begotten, not made." What is the point of this language? It is intended to assert an equality of being. Christians needed a language that enabled them to distinguish the Son from the Father while yet asserting that Father and Son shared equally in the divine life and were equal in dignity. For that, the language of "making" would not suffice. What we make, the product of our will, is not our equal. And so early Christians came to say that the Son is eternally begotten of the Father. This makes him unlike any other human being. Human beings are not begotten of God in the absolute sense that the Son is begotten of the Father. Human beings are made by God through human begetting. Hence, although we are not God's equals, we are of equal dignity with each other. We are therefore not at each other's disposal.

What is at stake, therefore, is the relation between the generations. Josef Pieper, the late German philosopher, once wrote that to love is to say, "It's good that you exist." To see our children as the products of our will—not just as those engendered by us but as those made by us—is to begin to lose the capacity to accept the next generation with surprise and with a kind of unlimited readiness to love.

I said at the outset that I would use Christian insights to try to articulate some of the underlying reasons for a rather widespread uneasiness about cloning. This is what I have tried to do by using the language of the Nicene Creed to speak of the meaning of persons in relation. Beginning from that particular starting point, I have sought to open up a vision of what it means to be human.

There is nothing automatic or guaranteed about such an understanding of our humanity. We can lose it, but then we lose some truly humane wisdom about the relation between the generations. That would be a high price to pay for the supposed benefits of cloning.

7

Seeking the Significant in the Factual

Nancy J. Duff

The case against cloning is not helped, Nancy Duff believes, by misunderstandings of the science or by pitting science against religion. The task is to get the details right, but even more to learn to recognize what is morally significant in the details. In particular, we need to look at how the technology of cloning lies within a culture that shapes its development according to its values. Christian theology enters the picture, not by prejudging the technology, but by lifting up the concern for the weak.

A few days after Ian Wilmut and Keith Campbell reported their success in cloning Dolly from an adult sheep, I wrote a theological response for a major newspaper.[1] Almost immediately I received letters challenging my position in startlingly contradictory ways. Those who wrote on behalf of science chastised me for *opposing* research into human cloning and promoting the superstitions of religious belief. Others, claiming to write on behalf of the church, upbraided me for *supporting* research into human cloning and promoting the interests of science over revelation. Many of these letters represented the stereotypical tension between science and religion. Journalists are often eager to exploit this tension and seem disappointed whenever scientists indicate interest in the perspective of religion or when theologians speak respectfully of scientists. Presenting science and

---

1. See the *Washington Post*, March 2, 1997, C1. Also, the first paragraph of this present essay (and the last two paragraphs) can be found in altered form in the Princeton Theological Seminary publication, *InSpire*, Summer 1997.

theology as opposing monoliths makes for more interesting report-ing and letter writing than does reflecting on the subtle and often cooperative relationship between them.

These journalists and my correspondents are not completely off course. Cooperation does exist between science and religion, but animosity lingers, too. Some Christians still claim that science con-tradicts the Bible and that the Bible always takes priority. Unfortunately, these religious critics of science are often woefully ignorant of the science they are rejecting or, for that matter, of the Bible they are defending. Consequently, scientists hesitate to pres-ent their work for public scrutiny for fear that "theologians" with little or no scientific background will automatically reject it by glibly accusing them of "playing God."

Scientists have every right to expect that anyone contributing to the moral assessment and regulation of scientific projects understand the basic science behind the research. Ian Wilmut and Keith Campbell correctly observe that for both science and ethics, "the details matter" because they are "at the heart of the science" and because "the facts of the case . . .bear upon ethical decisions and theological attitudes."[2] This is not to say that accurate knowledge of scientific discoveries and theories *alone* should dictate the church's moral stance, but we must admit that ignorance of these facts and theories does not lead to moral wisdom, either. Dietrich Bonhoeffer agreed:

> The best-informed man is not necessarily the wisest. Indeed there is the danger that precisely in the multiplicity of his knowledge he will lose sight of what is essential. But on the other hand, knowl-edge of an apparently trivial detail quite often makes it possible to see into the depths of things. And so the wise man will seek to acquire the best possible knowledge about events, but always with-out becoming dependent upon this knowledge. To recognize the significant in the factual is wisdom.[3]

2. Ian Wilmut and Keith Campbell, "So What Exactly Is a Clone?," in Ian Wilmut and Keith Campbell, and Colin Tudge, *The Second Creation: Dolly and the Age of Biological Control* (New York: Farrar, Straus and Giroux, 2000), 47.

3. Dietrich Bonhoeffer, *Ethics*, edited by Eberhard Bethge (New York: Macmillan, 1986), 68-69.

We cannot address the moral issues raised by science if the scientific details are poorly understood.

The field of science, on the other hand, must acknowledge its imperfect record in monitoring the professional behavior of scientists or the detrimental impact of some scientific endeavors on the well-being of individuals and on the common good of society. Some in science have pursued their work as if no moral considerations were even relevant to the pursuit of knowledge or its applications, almost as if science exists in some purely intellectual sphere in which it can enjoy immunity from *any* moral consideration. Others in the field of science argue that any moral implications science might have are beyond the ken of nonscientists, who cannot possibly earn the right to hold an opinion. Ethicists counter this notion by challenging the ethics licenses of the scientists, both sides thereby conspiring to reach an impasse in the roadway to finding "the significant in the factual."

Just how are we to engage scientists and ethicists (both secular and religious) in fruitful discussions of the morality of cloning? For some ethicists this discussion requires the identification of universal moral laws that can be equally well identified through both rational *and* religious arguments. This use of natural law, however, leads nonreligious participants in the conversation to suspect (rightly) that religious views have simply been disguised and promoted as the only views that coincide with reason and, therefore, as the only views that can legitimately claim to be universally binding. Conversely, the use of natural law can lead Christian participants to suspect (rightly) that their distinctive confession of faith in the living God who creates, redeems, and sustains life has been reduced to abstract principles that are subject to the dictates of human reason and common sense.

Rather than seek out universal laws, I believe the conversation about morally charged issues such as cloning should include careful listening to the various arguments, not because all views are equally valid, but because democracy demands that opposing positions be given a fair hearing. By the power of the Holy Spirit, coincidences will be found among the various positions, as will irreconcilable differences. For the sake of the common good, compromises will be hammered out in public policy and lines will be drawn where no compromise is possible. Certainly Christians can and will claim that the truth they hold is not simply relative to their community or merely subjective, but true for the world. Nevertheless, no claims for universally valid principles made by Christian theology and no heavy-handed claims that all right-minded individuals really agree with the Christian gospel, whether they realize it or not, should be allowed to shape public policy.

In the three years since Dolly debuted, I have found no compelling reasons for advancing the scientific possibility of *human* cloning. I disagree, however, with many of the arguments against human cloning offered in the public debate. As a theological ethicist, my concerns with arguments that ban human cloning for the wrong reasons include the accuracy of scientific information, on the one hand, and the formulation and use of Christian doctrine, on the other. Hence, attention is given first to correcting at least one error in the way people understand cloning, an error that functions as a premise to a flawed moral argument. Second, my focus shifts to some of the theological arguments employed in the debate.

MORAL ISSUES IN RELATION TO THE SCIENCE OF HUMAN CLONING

Although it is a daunting task for many nonscientists like myself to understand the basic scientific facts behind the sophisticated research involved in cloning, it is not impossible. One can begin by understanding why the cloning of Dolly represented such a scientific breakthrough. Dolly, after all, was not the first animal ever to be cloned. The *way* Dolly was cloned, however, shatters fundamental assumptions about mammalian and, therefore, human reproduction.

Although the term cloning is used primarily in public debate to refer to the work of scientists, cloning does occur naturally even within human reproduction. When the male gamete (sperm) fertilizes the female egg, a single-celled zygote is formed that contains within its nucleus all the genetic material (DNA) that will make up the entire newly developing individual. The genetic material within the nucleus duplicates itself and then divides, forming a two-celled blastocyst. This process of duplication and division continues until the multicelled blastocyst is implanted in the uterus (where-upon it is called an embryo). On occasion, however, before implantation takes place, not only do the cells within the blastocyst multiply, the blastocyst itself divides into two separate entities that are subsequently implanted in the uterus as two genetically identical embryos. Although we refer to these two individuals as identical twins, they are indeed clones.

For some time now animal cloning has been possible through a process known as "embryo splitting"; that is, one can divide the embryo into two identical embryos with the result of identical twins, just as in nature. With Dolly, however, an entirely different kind of cloning than embryo splitting was accomplished through a process called somatic cell nuclear transfer (SCNT). In this case, a body cell (a somatic cell) was taken from the mammary gland of a six-year-old ewe. Like almost every other cell within the body, this mammary gland cell carried within its nucleus the full genetic code for the entire animal, but only that part of the genetic material (DNA) that made it a mammary gland cell was "turned on." All of the other genetic material, though present, was "turned off" when the embryonic cells began to differentiate into various organs of the sheep's body. Until the cloning of Dolly, scientists thought that the DNA that had become quiescent in differentiated body cells could never be turned back on.

The scientists at Roslin Institute, however, found that if a differentiated body cell were deprived of nourishment for a period of time, eventually *the entire* DNA within the nucleus would become quiescent. In other words, the DNA that "told" this particular cell that it belonged to the mammary gland was "turned off," joining the other silent DNA contained within this cell. Next, the scientists at Roslin fused this quiescent body cell with the enucleated egg cell of another sheep (i.e., an egg cell that had its nucleus removed). When proper nutrients were restored to this quiescent cell and the necessary protein was provided by the enucleated egg cell, the resulting fused cell was brought to the point of totipotency, the condition that exists prior to cell differentiation. It then behaved like any embryo, moving through the processes of cell division, differentiation, and development. What is, of course, strikingly different about this embryo, which was implanted in the uterus of a third sheep and developed into Dolly, is that it was not formed from a fertilized egg.

What is now possible for sheep may soon be possible for human beings. If this is so, cloning by somatic cell nuclear transfer will sidestep what was once believed an absolute necessity for human reproduction, namely, the joining together of an egg and a sperm. Although males could be cloned (the somatic cell could be donated by a man), no contribution from a male is *necessary* for cloning, whereas contribution from the female (the enucleated egg cell) is necessary for cloning by SCNT to work. Theoretically, one woman could donate both a somatic cell and an enucleated egg, have the embryo that results from the fusing of these two cells implanted in her uterus, give birth to and become the social parent of the resulting child, who would be her genetic clone. Hence, as others have pointed out, new meaning could be given to the term "single parent." Genetically, of course, the cloned child would inherit the combined DNA of the woman's parents and would to a certain extent be rightly understood as the woman's delayed twin.

Of course, so much attention has been given to this startling possibility of human cloning by SCNT that we often overlook the other remarkable implications of the successful cloning of Dolly. Ian Wilmut points out that cloning is only one of three significant branches of research in biotechnology, with genetic engineering and genomics constituting the other two. Together these three technologies hold enormous potential for alleviating human suffering, but arguments against *human* cloning can, directly or indirectly, be used against all advancing technologies in genetics. Some critics of human cloning are convinced that all research in genetics has *human* cloning as its goal.

Ian Wilmut and Keith Campbell are not, however, seeking to advance the science of embryology for the purpose of cloning human beings. They are instead working within the realm of transgenic animals—animals that carry the gene of another species. The scientists at Roslin sought to produce transgenic sheep that express milk containing a human protein. Milk from these transgenic animals will be used to address devastating human maladies such as cystic fibrosis, diabetes, emphysema, and hemophilia.[4] Cloning by

---

4. Ian Wilmut, "The Importance of Being Dolly," in Wilmut, Campbell, and Tudge, *The Second Creation*, 19.

somatic cell nuclear transfer makes the proliferation of transgenic animals more efficient than traditional breeding. Nevertheless, for some people no disclaimer will convince them that human cloning is not the final goal of all work on cloning animals. For them, the "slippery slope" argument looms large. They fear that if we allow any research into cloning we will careen toward the inevitable worst-case scenarios, such as the mass replication of human beings for truly diabolical purposes. Of course, the slippery slope argument can work in reverse: opposition to human cloning could lead to opposition to *all* scientific research into cloning and related technologies, which in turn could prolong the suffering of those whose lives would benefit from such research.

Despite the intentions of Dolly's makers, public attention has focused almost entirely on human cloning, and popular misunderstandings of biology have distorted the arguments against it. For instance, some people hold the false impression that the cloned individual would in some way *be the same person* as the "parent clone." In truth, a human clone could not appear as a fully developed copy of the individual from whom he or she was cloned, but would come into the world as a newborn and move through the stages of infancy, childhood, adolescence, and so on, like everyone else. Furthermore, the traumas and joys of the "parent clone" would not be stored within the memory of the cloned individual any more than any parent's memories reside within a newborn. Because the environment and the experiences of the cloned child will be different from the "parent clone," personality traits, not to mention behavior, will be different. Environmental influences and mutations could also result in stark differences in appearance from the "parent clone" as well as the development of an entirely different set of talents.

Cloning a child, therefore, would *not* reverse the unbearable tragedy of losing a child. Parents who understand that might be less anxious to ask for cloning. Ian Wilmut reports that he met this expectation immediately:

> I fielded many of the telephone calls that flooded into Roslin Institute in the days after we went public with Dolly, and quickly came to dread the pleas from bereaved families, asking if we could

clone their lost loved ones. I have two daughters and a son of my own and know that every parent's nightmare is to lose a child and what parents would give to have them back, but I had and have no power to help. . . . Such pleas are based on a misconception: that cloning of the kind that produced Dolly confers an instant, exact replication—a virtual resurrection. This simply is not the case.[5]

A clone of the child who died would very likely look like the lost child and share many traits, but would not *be* the same individual with the same memories, talents, and preferences. The similarity between the cloned child and the child who died could increase the tendency to mistake the second child for the first, while differences exhibited in the second child could be experienced as enormous disappointments to those who intended this child to replace the first. In fact, the second child could no more replace the first child than giving birth to any second child could ever replace the one who had died. Correcting this misconception provides tools for insisting that if a child is born as a result of SCNT, she must be respected as the unique individual she is.

Some ethicists, such as Leon Kass, believe that insisting on this independent identity for a cloned individual constitutes a self-serving argument for the proponents of cloning:

> Since the birth of Dolly, there has been a fair amount of doubles-peak on the matter of genetic identity. Experts have rushed in to reassure the public that the clone would in no way be the same person or have any confusions about his identity; . . . They are pleased to point out that the clone of Mel Gibson would not be Mel Gibson. Fair enough. But one is shortchanging the truth by emphasizing the additional importance of the intrauterine environment, rearing, and social setting: genotype obviously matters plenty. That, after all, is the only reason to clone, whether human beings or sheep. The odds that clones of Wilt Chamberlain will play in the NBA are, I submit, infinitely greater than they are for clones of Robert Reich.[6]

---

5. Ibid.
6. Leon R. Kass, "The Wisdom of Repugnance," in Leon R. Kass and James Q. Wilson, *The Ethics of Human Cloning* (Washington, D.C. The American Enterprise Institute Press, 1998), 34.

While Kass correctly points to the almost inevitable tendency for parents and others to shape the cloned child "after the original— or at least to view the child with the original version always firmly in mind,"[7] he not only judges such tendencies to be inappropriate, he inadvertently condemns the cloned individual to such a destiny. Kass comes close to suggesting that one would *correctly* mistake the cloned individual for the parent clone when he remarks that "the cloned individual . . . will be saddled with a genotype that has already lived," as if this individual's body had already experienced life before she was born! Each individual life is an *unrepeatable* interplay between genes and environment. By insisting that an individual's "genetic distinctiveness and independence are the natural foreshadowing of the deep truth that they have their own and never-before-enacted life to live," Kass suggests that cloned individuals would *not have* "their own and never-before-enacted life to live," not only because third parties would prevent it, but because sharing a genotype with another makes one less of an individual human being.[8] As Karen Lebacqz has remarked, "If each twin—and even each personality of conjoined twins who share one body—is considered unique and protectable as a person with rights, then there is no reason to presume that a clone would not be unique and protectable as a person with rights."[9] One would not want the legitimate concerns expressed by ethicists such as Kass to be understood as so inevitable that nothing could be done to protect the cloned child from such attitudes.

THEOLOGICAL REFLECTIONS ON HUMAN CLONING

Searching for "the significant in the factual" begins as we look at the possibilities provided by the science of cloning, but for Christians, theological insights are necessary for discerning what is essential. Certainly, the fields of science and public policy are not required to appreciate the theological insights of Christians. Theological argu-

---

7. Ibid., 33-34.

8. Ibid, 41.

9. Karen Lebacqz, "Genes, Justice, and Clones," in Ronald Cole-Turner, editor, *Human Cloning: Religious Responses*, (Louisville, KY.: Westminster John Knox Press, 1997), 50.

ments do, however, make their way into the public debate, and while Christian belief cannot appropriately be imposed on the formation of public policy, it can be presented within the public debate along-side competing (and sometimes similar) arguments. Christians, therefore, need to formulate their theological understanding of human cloning and then carefully consider how theological language can responsibly be presented in the public arena of ideas.

"God above will not tolerate cloning of any kind," asserted one of my letter-writing friends. Is human cloning theologically intolerable, an affront to God? Is it "playing God"? Did Wilmut and Campbell already cross that line with Dolly? To answer these questions we must ask what it means to "play God." Kass implies that it means replacing nature or God's creation with human manufacture:

> Dolly was, quite literally, made. She is the work not of nature or nature's God but of man, an Englishman, Ian Wilmut and his fellow scientists. What is more, Dolly came into being not only asexually—ironically, just like "He [who] calls Himself a Lamb"—but also as the genetically identical copy (and the perfect incarnation of the form or blueprint) of a mature ewe, of whom she is a clone. . . . Now, by means of cloning, we may both [lambs and human beings] spring from the hand of man playing at being God.[10]

But surely we must never confuse humanity's *attempt* to usurp the place of God with humanity's ability to *succeed* at taking God's place. Only God creates. That is no less true if we are successful at cloning a human being. The first account of creation in Genesis claims that "in the beginning God created," and biblical scholarship shows that only "God" can be used as subject for the Hebrew word "create." The biblical account insists that human beings, though certainly creative, inventive, skillful at building, and astonishingly successful at uncovering the mysteries of life, *cannot* create as God does. The affirmation that God alone is the subject of the verb for create constitutes not a prohibition but a statement of a truth we cannot change. Human beings *cannot* take the place of God the Creator. If we label one born to a single mother as a "bastard child" (as Kass does) or wonder if a cloned child would have

---

10. Kass, "The Wisdom of Repugnance," 3-4.

a soul, we deny what theology affirms; namely, no matter what the circumstances of a child's birth, that child is a child of God.

Another argument that assigns human cloning to the human attempt to "play God" insists that human cloning denies the divinely established and eternally fixed essential meaning of procreation and the family. The Roman Catholic Church, for instance, officially objects to any human reproduction that does not result from sexual intercourse between a husband and wife who are open to the possibility of conceiving, bearing, and raising the child who may result from that sexual activity. Aside from what most critics think, Catholic tradition does allow for the unitive function of sexual intercourse; hence, couples beyond childbearing age and infertile couples are not prohibited from sexual intimacy. But for Roman Catholics the unitive function is never *morally* severed from the procreative function, even if procreation is not physically possible. A married couple engages in sexual intercourse open to the possibility of the pregnancy that may occur if natural circumstances do not prohibit it. Although such arguments reflect serious commitment to ensuring that children are conceived in love and welcomed into a family, these arguments go too far when they insist that children born outside this divinely established pattern are born in "an absence of love," as David M. Byers suggests,[11] or that a cloned child could be loved but not as a true son or daughter, as Brent Waters proposes:

> I am not saying I could not love or care for my clone. I think I could. I simply do not know how our relationships could be defined within the context of a family. We would both be deprived of a full sense of familial relatedness and belonging. For it is the distinctive character of the spousal, parental, filial, and sibling relationships, which shapes the ordering of a family's natural and social affinity. Cloning oneself could only distort the distinctive, though integrally related, familial roles by negating the boundaries separating and delimiting the roles of parent, child and sibling.[12]

11. David M. Byers, "An Absence of Love," in Cole-Turner, *Human Cloning*, 66-77.

12. Brent Waters, "One Flesh? Cloning, Procreation, and the Family," in Cole-Turner, *Human Cloning*, 84-85.

Unquestionably by virtue of bringing about a delayed twin, cloning confuses familial roles. Is the "parent clone" a parent or a sibling? What if the "parent clone" is herself an infant? Nevertheless, a child does not have to be born into a family to be loved and welcomed and to belong to that family in the same way as any son or daughter. Ironically, this essentialist argument regarding sexuality and familial relationships supports the argument *for* human cloning. The desire to have children of our own, when our own children are strictly understood as those biologically and genetically our heirs, *increases* the desire (now often defined as a need and a right) for access to new technologies that address rising cases of infertility. The possibility that human beings can be born through a process other than the fertilization of an egg by a sperm does not mean that human beings will have taken God's place as the Creator, Redeemer, and Sustainer of life. Furthermore, no person, including a cloned individual, can legitimately be denied the status of one who is created in God's image and is a child of God.

If cloning can rightly be considered as the human attempt to play God, that attempt is best understood as the prospect human cloning provides for exploiting human beings, especially those who are assigned to "the underside" of human history. Christian faith in God's incarnation in Jesus Christ who died on the cross leads to an overriding concern for those who are vulnerable and for those who suffer. We are even told in Matthew 25 that what we do for the least of our brothers and sisters, such as feeding the hungry, we do for Christ. Our love for God and our compassion for the most vulnerable neighbor cannot be separated. Hence, issues of racism, especially in light of previous historical attempts at eugenics, must not be ignored in our discussions of human cloning, though they are so rarely raised. Similarly, issues of the appropriate allocation of medical and technological resources must be addressed in light of the potential use of cloning for infertility rather than its promise for treating devastating human diseases and disabilities. Even so, Peter Paris correctly affirms the ongoing need for the church to remain in open conversation with science:

> Unlike Prometheus, no modern scientist has stolen anything from heaven. Rather, the capacity for knowledge has been graciously given to humanity by the omniscient and omnipotent Creator of us

all, the one whose authority and being are not usurped even by the
capacity of the creature to clone itself.[13]

I hope the church will welcome the opportunity to analyze the
complex moral challenges provided by recent advances in genetic
research. Before we are too quick to condemn all scientific efforts
at cloning, we ought to accept this opportunity to learn about the
incredible advances in science and marvel at the makeup of human
biology and human ingenuity. Far from challenging Christian
faith, such an exploration can lead to a richer appreciation of the
mysteries and wonders of God's creation. On the other hand,
before we are too quick to support the advances in science without
qualification ("Science is always a positive influence in the long
run," claimed another correspondent.), we must demonstrate the
ability to face honestly the potential for harm that inevitably
accompanies the potential for good in scientific advances.

Rather than becoming blindly enamored with exciting scientific discoveries, we cannot lose sight of other seemingly mundane
problems that lead to human suffering (such as the lack of fundamental health care experienced by millions of children and adults
in this country and abroad). The church does not have to assume
the stance of enemy in relation to science or biotechnology as it
has so often in the past, nor does the church have to be a naive or
uncritical ally of science and business. As the church continues to
participate in the conversation and debate over the moral issues
involved in human genetic research, as well as in plant and animal
genetic research, we cannot assume that all scientists or leaders in
the biotechnology industry are devoid of moral concerns, nor can
we simply let science and business regulate themselves. We have
the opportunity for genuine and fruitful conversation with the scientific and business worlds involved in genetic research. We can
maintain our own distinct identity as the church while avoiding
moral pronouncements that are devoid of scientific knowledge.

---

13. Peter J. Paris, "A View from the Underside," in Cole-Turner, *Human
Cloning*, 48.

8

Cloning and Sin: A Niebuhrian Analysis and a Catholic, Liberationist Response

Lisa Sowle Cahill

The debate over the ethics of cloning is too often limited to the concerns of individuals. Should parents be free to choose it? Will children be harmed by it? Lisa Sowle Cahill challenges us to broaden the scope of our thinking and to see cloning in its context of social and economic justice. What is cloning for and who will benefit from this new form of "marketed reproduction"? Will it not lead to greater injustice, and must we not in fact call this injustice sin? In the face of institutional powers made more powerful by technology, can we still strive for a just society?

The terms of the public policy debate in the United States have until now been too narrow to permit any serious critique of the marketing of cloning and other genetic innovations, much less the reversal of this trend. Ethical analysis of cloning tends to focus on national policy only, to be individualistic and pragmatic, and to accept that a market economy can serve as the key social institution for allocating medical resources.

Within these narrow limits, many have looked at cloning as a possible expression of hubris, a violation of created limits, and a social danger insofar as it disrupts natural family relationships and objectifies reproduction and children.[1] Yet cloning is rarely

---

1. See Oliver O'Donovan, *Begotten or Made?* (Oxford: Clarendon, 1984); Gilbert Meilaender, "Begetting and Cloning," in Gregory E. Pence, editor, *Flesh of My Flesh: The Ethics of Cloning Humans* (Lanham, Md., and Oxford: Rowman and Littlefield, 1998), 39-44; and Brent Waters, "One Flesh? Cloning,

considered from the standpoint of social justice across class and economic lines.[2] The premise of this essay is that cloning, as a problem of social ethics, should be more fully considered in light of the Christian doctrine of sin. The record of the global life sciences industries suggests that the development of cloning, like other new genetic technologies, will be dominated by the industrialized nations, to the benefit of investors and those who can afford access to the results. These beneficiaries show little regard for the effect on human welfare across a society or globally. The approval of cloning needs to be placed in a broader social context. Christian views of sin can help elucidate the dynamics of biotechnology investment and use, while opening a window onto possible remedies.

Three important cultural factors have contributed to this situation. First, the guiding moral value in our political culture is autonomous freedom, bestowed, in the case of biotechnology, on client and provider, and on science and business. The idea that free, self-interested behavior, subjected to a minimum of social restraint, ultimately will benefit society, is a counterpart of the high priority we place on freedom as a moral and social value. So both our economy and our politics are governed by the near absolutization of freedom.

Second, disproportionate importance is assigned to scientific rationality as a moral methodology. Scientific method privileges logical deduction from established premises, empirical verification of hypotheses, concrete results, and the immediate application of knowledge. An assumption virtually unquestioned by either the defenders or the detractors of cloning is that its morality ultimately comes down to the possibility of showing that cloning is intrinsically immoral, either because every instance will demonstrably violate the freedom of individuals (or their individuality, an apparent precondition of freedom); or because it involves specific physical or psychological harm or great risk of harm. If neither of these outcomes can be shown beyond reasonable doubt, then cloning should not be prohibited. Individual purveyors and clients should

Procreation, and the Family," in Ronald Cole-Turner, editor, *Human Cloning: Religious Responses* (Louisville, Ky.: Westminster John Knox Press, 1997), 78-90.

2. See Karen Lebacqz, "Genes, Justice, and Clones," in Cole-Turner, *Human Cloning,* 56. For social justice analyses of genetics in general, see Ted Peters, editor, *Genetics: Issues of Social Justice* (Cleveland: Pilgrim Press, 1998).

be free to perfect, provide, and purchase cloning. Approaches to values and to society that are more inductive, more affective, more long range, and less conclusive have much less persuasive power in a culture that values clear evidence and immediate outcomes over gradual consensus building and incremental social results.

Third, scientists and corporate investors in the United States are well positioned to market cloning and other biotechnologies both nationally and globally. Hence there is an immense economic incentive to avoid or reduce restraints on research. In 1989 and 1990, James Watson argued to Congress that the Human Genome Project be funded specifically on the grounds that what is good for U.S. business is good for the nation.[3] Those already in decision-making and leadership roles in science and public policy stand to gain profits, prestige, and power from the pursuit of cloning. This creates a powerful bias against restrictive policies such as a permanent ban, a bias that affects public moral reasoning as typically undertaken by national policy advisory bodies.

An illustration is the recommendation of the National Bioethics Advisory Commission that "reproductive" cloning be banned only temporarily. After presenting this recommendation, I will turn to Reinhold Niebuhr for a broader, more nuanced interpretation of wrong behavior as injustice. Niebuhr's interpretation of sin as pride and sensuality, and his concept of social sin as collective egotism, may be illuminating for the cloning debate. Niebuhr's analysis of the dynamics of sin can be complemented by the response to sinfulness of the Roman Catholic justice tradition. On the one hand, Niebuhr is convinced that social change will not come about without some form of coercion that forces power elites to forgo a portion of their prerogatives. On the other hand, Catholic social ethics holds out hope of civil, public discourse that can bring all social groups together to serve the common good. Influenced by liberation theology, recent Catholic teaching has put more emphasis on inclusive participation in defining the common good, so that those formerly excluded can share in the reconstitution of the social order, and not merely stand as the beneficiaries of authorities who claim to act on their behalf.

---

3. Karen Lebacqz, "Fair Shares: Is the Genome Project Just?" in Peters, *Genetics,* 84.

Cloning as Biotechnology: Promises, Realities, and Public Ethics

Shortly after the sheep Dolly was cloned in 1997, U.S. president Bill Clinton asked the fifteen-member National Bioethics Advisory Commission to advise him on the ethics and policy of cloning. NBAC recommended that federal funding be withheld from so-called reproductive cloning (the attempt to bring a clone to birth) and that Congress enact a federal law against such cloning (not enacted as of 2000). It did not, however, ban research on nonhuman cloning or on cloning techniques, and even the ban on reproductive cloning was temporary and revisable. The main reason favoring the ban was the experimental nature of the technology and consequent risk to children born of it, conditions that might be ameliorated with time.

NBAC commendably conducted hearings in which many different viewpoints were represented, including those of religious traditions. The authors of NBAC's report, *Cloning Human Beings*, present the evidence in a rounded and balanced way. For example, the report acknowledges that cloning raises concerns about "manufacturing children according to specification," and registers a concern for the danger in "the dominance it introduces into the parent-child relationship," on account of which cloning "is viewed by many as fundamentally at odds with the acceptance, unconditional love, and openness characteristic of good parenting."[4] The report also considers the possibility of "an inappropriate use of scarce resources," diverted from "more pressing medical and social needs."[5]

In the end, however, such concerns about endangered social values like respect for persons (nonobjectification), family integrity, individuality, and distributive justice, were not sufficient to override "other important social values, such as protecting the widest possible sphere of personal choice, particularly in matters pertaining to procreation and child rearing, maintaining privacy and the freedom of scientific inquiry, and encouraging the possible development of new biomedical breakthroughs."[6] The report's resolution, a morato-

4. *Cloning Human Beings: Report and Recommendations of the National Bioethics Advisory Commission* (Rockville, Md., 1997), 69.

5. Ibid., 72.

6. Ibid., ii.

rium on reproductive cloning, may have been an attempt at a compromise position. The report did not attempt, however, to address the relative worth of a worldview in which both reproductive and scientific freedom are preferred to, say, access to basic medical care for all; or a vision of the good society in which family relationships are normally based on biological or marital kinship, compared to one in which family structure depends on individual choice. NBAC did take refuge in one reason for caution about cloning that seemed concrete and nonphilosophical: safety.[7] Physical risk to clones as a barrier to acceptance of cloning as a practice warranted NBAC's provisional ban, pending further investigation.

On the positive side of the risk-benefit calculus about cloning are the potential uses of cloning as an infertility therapy, as a means of bypassing genetic disease, or as a reproductive tool for individuals or same-sex couples, all of whom might want to avoid genetic input from an outsider. Cloning could also be used to provide a source of compatible tissue for a genetic twin; to reproduce a dead or dying loved one; or to allow a parent to select a desired genotype for a prospective child. Once the safety risk is reduced through experimentation on "nonreproductive" cloned embryos, pressure to remove the ban will increase. If neither NBAC nor our culture as a whole has engaged in a larger debate about the impact of cloning on the good life and the common good, then the worldview in which reproductive, scientific, and market freedom dominate is likely to win and cloning to become a reality. This is certainly the direction in which the profits from cloning research lie.

Enhancing profitability is the fact that cloning, for the above reasons, will be an exportable commodity, once it has been developed in the relatively unregulated U.S. environment, where embryos can be produced for research, as long as they are created with private and not public funds. It is not difficult to imagine cloning's appeal to wealthy infertile or genetically at-risk couples in cultures with more deeply rooted objections to involving donors, especially male donors, in the reproductive ventures of married couples heavily pressured to carry on the family line.

According to the 1999 United Nations *Human Development Report*:

---

7. Ibid., 65.

Globalization—and its new rules—is . . . shaping the path of new technologies. Over the past twenty years increasing privatization of research and development, ever-growing liberalization of markets and the tightening of intellectual property rights have set off a race to lay claim to knowledge, and this has changed technology's path. The risk is that poor people's and poor countries' interests are being left on the sidelines.[8]

It is likely that cloning research and development will confirm a pattern in which the technologies selected for funding and research attention will not be those that can serve the most basic needs of the majority of the world's population, but those that can serve the economic interests of those in possession of capital. Already, in the genetic engineering of agricultural products, more effort has gone into more profitable pest-resistant crops for Europe and North America than into drought-resistant crops that could help feed the starving of Africa. The major exporters of genetically altered food—the United States, Canada, Australia, Argentina, Uruguay, and Chile—campaigned successfully in February 1999 to block international safeguards required under the Biosafety Protocol of the Convention on Biological Diversity passed at the Rio de Janeiro Earth Summit in 1992. The impact of economic interests on national participation in international policy formation is likely to be equally large.

Cloning is not likely to become a reproductive or therapeutic means designed for the majority of the nation's or the world's population, and especially not for the least well off. To approve cloning may well be to threaten individuality, respect for persons, and the family; it is most certainly also to ratify vast social inequities already entrenched in the biomedical sphere. To reply that other reproductive technologies and other genetics-related therapies are already geared to making profits by serving the prosperous few is simply to continue to avoid the question of whether and how such techniques can be part of an ethically worthy society governed by norms of justice.

At stake is whether justice is concerned exclusively or primarily with individual freedoms, of investors, knowledge producers, technicians, and clients, for example. Or does justice also refer to respon-

---

8. United Nations Development Program, *Human Development Report 1999* (New York and Oxford: Oxford University Press, 1999), 66.

sibility to the common good, including access for all to the basic necessities of life, including medical care? Do justice and moral responsibility pertain only to one's own family, to one's local community, one's social class, or to the nation of which one is a citizen? Or do we bear some responsibility in justice, through international institutions, to persons in distant cultures, who may be affected by our actions? In the words of the theologian Diana Fritz Cates, "Being compassionate and just within our modern global context requires recognizing that every human being is a 'neighbor' who has some claim on us to be received and responded to with attention, affection, beneficence, respect, and fairness."[9] Or as stated by the philosopher Paul Ricoeur, a genuinely ethical perspective requires "aiming at the good life with and for others in just institutions."[10]

REINHOLD NIEBUHR

The justice and injustice of institutions constitutes the subject matter of social ethics. Reinhold Niebuhr links his Christian social ethics to a doctrine of sin. At the individual level, sin manifests itself as pride or sensuality. At the social level, sin, willful injustice, takes hold through the self-deceptive dynamics of collective egotism.

Wrong and unjust uses of cloning can be considered from a philosophical vantage point. What is provided by a religious one, calling injustice "sin," is the recognition that human behavior is accountable to standards whose foundations transcend history, human laws, and customs. Religion also explains that human behavior is liable to perversions whose origins escape rational analysis and defy attempts at moral reform. According to Niebuhr, sin originates in human finitude and becomes reality as the refusal to acknowledge dependence on God. "The religious dimension of sin is man's rebellion against God, his effort to usurp the place of God."[11] A similar line of objection to cloning has been taken frequently by those theological writers who see

9. Diana Fritz Cates, *Choosing to Feel: Virtue, Friendship, and Compassion for Friends* (Notre Dame, Ind.: University of Notre Dame Press, 1997), 202.

10. Paul Ricoeur, *Oneself as Another* (Chicago: University of Chicago Press, 1992), 180.

11. Reinhold Niebuhr, *The Nature and Destiny of Man*, volume I: *Human Nature* (New York: Charles Scribner's Sons, 1964), 179.

cloning as a violation of created nature and an abandonment of a vision of procreation as participation in God's creative act and ultimately as gift. One of the first to state this objection was Paul Ramsey, who saw asexual reproduction as depersonalizing and arrogant. He wrote that we should "procreate new beings like ourselves in the midst of our love for one another, and in this there is a trace of the original mystery by which God created the world because of his love."[12]

Less frequently noted in regard to cloning are the sentences following the one in which Niebuhr characterizes sin as "rebellion": "The moral and social dimension of sin is injustice. The ego which falsely makes itself the centre of existence in its pride and will-to-power inevitably subordinates other life to its will and thus does injustice to other life."[13] This side of sin, injustice to others that takes form systematically in structures of oppression, is coherent with biblical depictions, from the warnings of the prophets like Amos and Isaiah about powerful leaders and classes who neglect the poor, to the New Testament parable of judgment (Matthew 25), in which those who see themselves as righteous are indicted for neglect of the needy and are cast out from God's kingdom.

One of Niebuhr's particular contributions is his development of the social side of pride as injustice. Niebuhr explicates both the social effects of sin and the self-deception that enables it with the category "collective egotism." This term refers to the inclination of individuals to disguise self-interest by aligning selfish behavior with the welfare of a larger group of which they are members. Individuals sin when they cover their own self-assertion with defense of higher values or some larger collectivity. Such claims allow possibilities of self-aggrandizement that few individuals would dare to assert on their own.[14] In the case at hand, few researchers would advocate for unrestricted funds for cloning with the stated purpose of winning a Nobel prize, patenting a remunerative cloning process, or opening a vastly profitable international reproductive clinic. They might, on the other hand, advocate for the freedom of "science," hold up the "needs" and

---

12. Paul Ramsey, *Fabricated Man: The Ethics of Genetic Control* (New Haven: Yale University Press, 1970), 88.

13. Niebuhr, *Nature and Destiny of Man*, 88.

14. Ibid., 211-213.

"desperation" of the clientele they hope to attract, or simply allude to "vast potential benefits for mankind."

In addition to pride, according to Niebuhr, sin takes the form of "sensuality." Sensuality is the escape from freedom and the possibilities of the human spirit to find meaning in transcendent values. Sin as sensuality is "becoming lost in the detailed processes, activities and interests of existence, an effort which results inevitably in unlimited devotion to limited values."[15] Niebuhr also describes sensuality as losing oneself in "some natural vitality."[16] According to the biblical tradition, sin as pride is more basic than sin as sensuality, which is derivative. Sensuality can turn into the same "lust for power" that characterizes pride and that results in injustice.[17]

Pressure for the social legitimization of cloning can manifest sin as sensuality in two ways. Most obviously, the absolutization of either scientific research or profits, under the aegis of serving humanity, is a form of immersion in a conditioned value, unlimited dedication to which will result in a disproportion of human relationships and injustice to those who will be harmed by or excluded from pursuit of this ostensibly noble cause. Perhaps less obviously, the promotion of cloning as a benefit to infertile, genetically at-risk, or same-sex couples can represent a narrow fixation on the "natural vitality" of biological reproduction. Certainly a good, biological reproduction or genetic parenthood is not an absolute value. In fact, becoming a parent in general is not an absolute value, though it often seems to be constructed as such by infertility specialists and by infertile persons themselves, for whom the understandable quest for a biological child becomes all-consuming. Pertinent to cloning and other reproductive technologies, one can become a parent nonbiologically, through the adoption of one of the many existing children who are "unwanted" because of sex, age, or race. If the funds currently expended on cloning research were used to facilitate, supervise, and support appropriate adoption, the total impact on human happiness and the alleviation of suffering would multiply astronomically.

15. Ibid., 185.
16. Ibid., 186.
17. Ibid., 186-94.

As a Christian theologian, Niebuhr holds out greater hope of altruistic behavior and dedication to transcendent values for people of faith than for society at large. The highest possibility of social relations is mutually beneficial behavior, not true altruism. Thus, his solution to pride, sensuality, collective egotism, and the injustice they spawn is two fold. First, coercion is necessary to attain and maintain the balance of power that is the only effective restraint on unjust action. Niebuhr believes that moral persuasion will not be enough. Social institutions must be governed by principles of justice and civil laws that ensure equilibrium of power and the reciprocal relationships that constitute social justice.[18] Second, in addition to the benign coerciveness of just institutions and laws, Niebuhr believes that religiously inspired altruism or love as self-sacrifice must play a supportive and sustaining role. Love has a "dialectical" relationship to justice, inspiring and initiating justice, and always holding the justice attainable in human societies to a higher, transcendent standard.[19]

The dialectical relation of love and justice that Niebuhr recommends or discerns has been criticized for its paradoxical and unstable character. Niebuhr is a relative pessimist about the potential of human societies to engage in open, good-faith debate about the common good and to move consistently toward institutions that are more just and inclusive. An alternative position, one that is more optimistic and more confident that Christian ideals can be reflected in the public order, is the tradition of Catholic social teaching.

CATHOLIC SOCIAL ETHICS

For more than one hundred years, the Catholic popes have authored encyclical letters that address social organization and social justice in terms of "the common good."[20] In recent years, this tradition has been heavily influenced by the biblical commitment of liberation theology to make an "option for the poor." While justice requires that all share in and contribute to the common good, the option for

---

18. Reinhold Niebuhr, *The Nature and Destiny of Man*, volume II: *Human Destiny* (New York: Charles Scribner's Sons), 244-258.

19. Ibid., 247.

20. See John A. Coleman, S.J., editor, *One Hundred Years of Catholic Social Thought: Celebration and Challenge* (Maryknoll, N.Y.: Orbis Books, 1991).

the poor reminds us that those who have been most excluded are entitled to special compensatory efforts. Social institutions must equalize relationships that in the past have been distorted by sin, and this may require making amends for a history of unjust treatment. Unlike Niebuhr, the Catholic social tradition is confident not only that just social institutions can be created but that members of society can be persuaded to move from unjust to just treatment of others. Bias and selfishness can be overcome through reasonable persuasion and moral conversion. A just society is a historical possibility, even if the achievement of justice requires self-sacrifice and the relinquishing of prerogatives already enjoyed by the privileged.

An encyclical letter of John Paul II, *Gospel of Life*, can serve as an example. In this document, sin is identified with a "culture of death" in which persons are not respected in themselves, but for their usefulness to others. "This culture is actively fostered by powerful cultural, economic, and political currents which encourage an idea of society excessively concerned with efficiency."[21] In biomedical areas, including reproduction, life is instrumentalized, aggravated by a cultural climate that finds no meaning in suffering. Too often, procreation "expresses a desire or indeed the intention to have a child 'at all costs,' and not because it signifies the complete acceptance of the other and therefore an openness to the richness of life which the child represents."[22]

The pope is concerned with social relationships in the culture of death. He speaks of the need for more just local and international distribution of resources, and laments that

> Even in participatory systems of government, the regulation of interests often occurs to the advantage of the most powerful, since they are the ones most capable of maneuvering not only the levers of power but also of shaping the formation of consensus. In such a situation, democracy becomes an empty word.[23]

Yet humanity "is in no way predestined for evil."[24] That respect for the lives and well being of all, in a spirit of solidarity, should

---

21. John Paul II, *Evangelium Vitae* (*Gospel of Life*) Origins, 24:42 (1995): 694 (no. 12).

22. Ibid., 695 (no. 15), 698 (no. 23).

23. Ibid., 714 (no. 70).

24. Ibid., 693 (no. 8).

characterize any good society is a point the pope makes with both biblical images and philosophical argumentation. He gives examples of Jesus favoring the poor in his preaching and actions.[25] Yet the "gospel of life" is a message that can be read in human experience and human nature. It is a message for the whole of human society, for it defines the common good, including respect for human rights, especially the right to life, justice, and peace.[26] Its truth is not dependent on the Bible or revelation, but consists in "those essential and innate human and moral values which flow from the very truth of the human being and express and safeguard the dignity of the person."[27]

Although the Catholic Church's teaching on reproductive technologies is most known for its concern about the status of the embryo and the integrity of the marital sex act,[28] the social justice component is also important. Several Catholic authors have placed genetic technologies and cloning in the context of justice and the common good, following the lead of recent popes in understanding the common good globally.[29] The Brazilian theologian Marcio Fabrî dos Anjos, who has also been a member of the Brazilian National Commission for Ethics in Research, speaks of human interconnectedness and the need for solidarity. To overcome colonialism and dependency, and prevent them from dominating the organization of biotechnology and genetic research, knowledge, not just products, must be shared, and the needs of social groups, not just the rights of individual research subjects or clients, must be taken into account. "We need to have the courage to confront also the tacit laws of the political, economic and cultural colonial-

25. Ibid., 701 (no. 32).

26. Ibid., 724 (no. 101).

27. Ibid., 714 (no. 71).

28. Congregation for the Doctrine of the Faith, *Donum Vitae* (*Instruction on Respect for Human Life in its Origin and on the Dignity of Procreation: Replies to Certain Questions of the Day*) Origins 16/40 (1987) 697-711.

29. See, for example, the articles by Cahill, Clague, Fabri, and Ryan in Maureen Junker-Kenny and Lisa Sowle Cahill, editors, *The Ethics of Genetic Engineering, Concilium* 1998/2 (London and Maryknoll, N.Y.: SCM Press/ Orbis Books, 1998).

ism to which most poor countries are still subject."[30] Laws and policies should be revised on the basis of consultation that involves the poor as agents, not mere recipients of the compassion of those who currently hold the reins of power.

The reorganization of the international regulation of the life sciences industries is obviously an enormous and enormously complicated problem. But it can be stated briefly that Catholic social ethics supports three characteristics of reform also advocated by other groups and authors: solidarity with, compassion toward, and empowerment of the exploited and dispossessed; policies, directives, and laws generated at both the local, indigenous, level, and at the international or global level; and a serious commitment to make better and more cooperative regulation a reality. Cultures must develop appropriate regulation of biotechnology based on their native values and the needs of their populations; from the other side, international cooperation is necessary to channel and control the actions of multinational scientific and business ventures, from the Human Genome Project to private companies. For instance, Merck Pharmaceuticals, without regulation, has made an agreement with the Costa Rica National Institute of Biodiversity to pay $1.1 million for access to 10,000 plant and insect samples, and to pay royalties if its research leads to a successful drug.[31] Reproductive technologies are scarcely regulated at all in the United States, which makes this an environment of choice for researchers and entrepreneurs, and a useful base from which to develop and export the profit-making potential of cloning. But Christian social ethics recognizes the potential for sin to pervert the discussion, analysis, and implementation of cloning, and the need to develop national and global institutions that can deal effectively with this negative potential.

CONCLUSION

As is the case with other forms of biotechnology and genetic engineering, cloning needs to be examined within a Christian perspective that takes sin seriously, recognizes sin's social dimensions and

---

30. Marcio Fabrî dos Anjos, "Power, Ethics, and the Poor in Human Genetic Research," in Junker-Kenny and Cahill, *Ethics of Genetic Engineering*, 79.

31. United Nations Development Program, *Human Development Report*, 71.

its intransigence, and moves decisively nonetheless to propose more just social structures. In such a perspective, cloning as a practice may be judged to be a form of social sin or injustice, even if not every instance of cloning is demonstrably wrong or harmful. A pattern of behavior has greater social effects than isolated instances (on the family, on attitudes toward children, and on biomedical resource allocation, for example). Moreover, cloning as a type of human reproduction is also a type of biotechnology destined for the market. The fact that individual decisions to clone may be carried out with good motives and results does not obviate the danger in the larger picture.

Finally, an approach to moral analysis modeled on the empirical and deductive model of modern science will of its nature tend to seek generalizations that can be applied to every case and that are backed up by incontrovertible, factual evidence. While this kind of moral reasoning can be helpful, it is not sufficient, as classical ethical appeals to virtue, prudence, ideals of human flourishing, and visions of the good suggest. Evaluating the wrongness or injustice of cloning, considered as a novel social practice of marketed reproduction, and not only as a new category of what ultimately remain individual actions, requires a stance of moral discernment that stretches beyond logical analysis and scientific estimates of risk. It must rely in part on reflection and imagination concerned with the human good and the good society. An ethical appraisal of cloning must draw on positive experiences and ideals of the good, on negative contrast experiences both real and imagined, on affective responses to value, and on prudent recognition of the mean between extremes. Christian symbolism of sin, redemption, and the reign of God can foster these ideals, responses, and recognition. Christian symbols can also resonate with and stimulate the moral imagination and perception of members of other traditions who likewise seek the common good.

9

Contingency, Tragedy, and the Virtues of Parenting

Sondra Wheeler

Parenting is a risky undertaking that requires moral character, and we need to consider carefully whether reproductive cloning threatens to undermine the virtues that are necessary for parenting. To be a parent requires that we face risk with unconditional love, courage, and generosity. Wheeler asks us to think how cloning might change fundamentally the relationship between parent and child, leading finally to what she calls "a basic distortion of parenting."

The immediate furor sparked by the birth of Dolly the cloned sheep has now died down. We have turned our attention to other things, perhaps revealing that as a nation we have the cultural equal of attention deficit disorder. More deeply, I suspect, we have run out of things to say about human cloning, and this is the reflection of our lack of a shared and generally available language in which to talk about our hopes, fears, and intuitions concerning the control of human genetic inheritance.

Discussion continues, mostly in specialized settings, academic and professional contexts, or scientific and philosophical journals. There, experts debate the possible benefits and foreseeable risks of cloning applications that would result in the birth of a child who was the deliberate genetic copy of some existing template, whether of one of the rearing parents or of some other person. These discussions are important. It is quite reasonable to look to scientists and ethicists to help us understand the technical possibilities, and to frame the questions that the fast-maturing discipline of bioethics teaches us to ask about their moral acceptability. But such debates among specialists are not sufficient.

All proposed forays into human genetic engineering are significant because they have the capacity, by changing what we *do*, to change what we *mean* by terms as basic as mother and father. Accepting such new practices requires us to make a subtle shift in what we understand and intend in entering into the most fundamental of all human relationships, that between parent and child. There is no academic specialty in what it means to be the fruit of the previous generation or the progenitors of the next. No degrees are available that confer the wisdom necessary to judge the terms on which, or the ends *for* which, we ought to undertake to determine the genetic complement of those other human beings whom we will call our children. Moreover, whether they realize it or not, there are no human beings on the planet to whom the moral character of these basic social ties is irrelevant. Therefore it is important to continue the discussion in the broadest possible terms and among the widest possible segment of the society that stands to be affected by these developments.

My intention here is to explore the implications of human reproductive cloning for our understanding of the relationship between parents and children. I propose to do this in a language as close as I can manage to the ordinary terms in which people think about their own relationships with their parents and their children. I want to talk about certainty and uncertainty, about control and randomness, and about the interplay of power and helplessness that are part of the ordinary experience of conceiving, bearing, and raising children. I want to talk about how we make moral judgments about the use of power in this realm. And whether I want to or not, I will be forced to talk about suffering, about how we as human beings can and should respond to it.

However, before entering on that extended reflection, I will begin by reviewing some of the things that have been said about the possibility of cloning, by those in favor of it and by those deeply opposed to it. I do this to capture something of the flavor of the public conversation, the concerns that have animated it, and the reasons that have been offered for and against cloning human beings. Against this background, I will be in a position to consider whether the character of parenting as a moral practice has received enough attention within this discussion.

REVISITING THE ARGUMENTS FOR CLONING

Positive arguments for human reproductive cloning are actually hard to come by. Those who support the pursuit of that goal[1] generally do so for what might be called negative reasons (that is, they find no convincing reasons to ban the practice) rather than for the sake of some particular good cloning is expected to bring about. There are, in fact, a number of rationales for supporting cloning of preimplantation embryos as a tool in basic and clinical research, and a wide range of possible therapeutic benefits projected to come from such research. But these do not depend upon implanting cloned embryos or the result of nuclear transfers and bringing them to term, and thus do not fall into the category of reproductive cloning. Just to be clear, there are also serious arguments against these research protocols, rooted in respect for the embryo as a form of nascent human life that should not be manipulated and discarded. These objections, however, are not particular to procedures that involve cloning, applying as well to any creation of human embryos not destined for implantation.

Some of the arguments that have been made in favor of reproductive cloning proceed on libertarian grounds, that only direct and demonstrated harm to a recognized other should limit individual autonomy. These depend on the supposition that the procedure can be made safe for the cloned child-to-be and for the gestating mother, and on the prior supposition that failures on the way to such a technical development do not harm any being who is morally eligible for protection. On these premises, libertarians argue that no one has the right to limit what researchers or prospective cloners wish to

---

1. Estimates of the likelihood of overcoming the practical barriers to human cloning, and of the time frame needed to do so, vary widely. All informed sources agree, however, that we are still some distance scientifically from the possibility.

do. Cloning is to be supported because it might provide a way for prospective parents to obtain the offspring they want, whether that means overcoming disease or just exercising "quality control." The substantive good in view in this position is thus individual liberty.

Most people do not find such arguments for unconstrained cloning convincing on the face of it, for the same reason that they do not find libertarian arguments in favor of ending tax support for public education convincing. It is entirely too evident how much common stake we all have in the bearing and upbringing of children, who are after all destined to be our neighbors and inheritors, to suppose that such practices should be matters of purely private judgment. Even those who have supported some uses of human cloning have generally recognized that proposals must pass greater public scrutiny than this.

More appealing to some have been arguments based on benefits that might be obtained using this technique for individuals in particular circumstances. Rabbi Moshe Tendler, for example, envisions a case in which someone, all of whose relatives were killed in the Holocaust, is unable to produce gametes, but has a great stake in continuing his or her family line.[2] The use of nuclear transfer cloning technology might allow this person to have posterity by first producing a genetic twin. Ronald Cole-Turner asks whether a couple who loses a late-term pregnancy at a point when they can no longer conceive might be justified in cloning the dead fetus to obtain a child who was genetically related to both of them.[3] A number of commentators have proposed that cloning might enable couples who carry certain serious genetic defects to be certain of not passing these to their offspring. And a few have noted that cloning could allow lesbian couples to have children genetically related to them and to no one else, extending the contemporary notion of a right to procreate to those now excluded by biology. These are not, of course, routine circumstances, and such unusual scenarios raise the question of whether "hard cases" make better ethics than they do law. But the exploration of quandaries

---

2. In the unpublished proceedings of a public forum on cloning at the American Association for the Advancement of Science in June 1997.

3. In private correspondence, June 2000.

can help to clarify what is at the heart of our intuitions and our considered judgments and help us articulate what might be at stake in our decisions. I will return to such particular justifications for reproductive cloning near the end of the discussion.

ARGUMENTS AGAINST CLONING

Arguments against the moral permissibility of cloning can also be divided into types. The first and simplest type argues on grounds of scientific safety and reliability that such experimental procedures are too risky to apply to human beings. Those who would make this the grounds for an ongoing or permanent ban contend that any research that would reduce the uncertainty is morally prohibited because it would involve helpless and unconsenting subjects in high-risk, non-therapeutic research. They deny that animal studies can ever give us sufficient confidence to justify proceeding to human trials.

Many have objected to cloning because they see a threat to human dignity and individuality in a technique that creates a genetic replica of an existing genotype. Popular commentators have raised questions about the personal identity, value, and social status to be accorded a clone. While others counter that cloning poses no greater threat to genetic uniqueness than natural twinning, opponents point to a distinction between what one accepts as a random event and what one sets out to do. They also point out that it makes a difference if one of the twins is a deliberately chosen template, already fully developed, who may function socially as the "parent" of the other.

Related but distinct are the concerns of those who worry about compromising genetic diversity in favor of the replication of a few highly valued genotypes. Along with the biological risks if it were to be done on a large scale, cloning raises philosophical questions about human nature and the value of human differences. Further along this same trajectory of concern for human freedom and dignity, some have speculated about the uses of cloning to create whole categories of people specially adapted for some social purpose, ranging from soldiers to worker drones to sources of "replacement parts" for their cloners. Some have proposed these possibilities with full seriousness as moral barriers to the application of this technique to human beings. Whatever the criteria or motives for selection, the replication of a desirable genotype has seemed to many to be a fatal step toward treating infants as commodities.

CHANGING THE FOCUS

Common to all these objections is the fear of making a human being a merely instrumental good, a being created at someone else's direction and to his or her specifications to fulfill a human purpose outside the child's own flourishing. This is seen as a basic violation of the duty of respect for persons, which forbids treating them solely as means to other ends, rather than as ends in themselves. This concern is evident even among those thinkers, both religious and secular, who do not find the asexual character of replication and the lack of genetic uniqueness compelling arguments against cloning. Ted Peters, for example, untroubled by these issues, nevertheless worries that "reproduction will come to look more and more like production . . .with quality control and babies will come to look more and more like products."[4] Karen Lebacqz, in considering sympathetically whether cloning might serve social justice by extending the putative right to a genetically related child to disadvantaged groups, asks a more basic question: "Is there something fundamentally flawed with the notion that children must be genetically ours? Is the very language of 'rights' out of place when it comes to procreation and families?" She concludes: "Our individualistic, 'rights'-based assumptions about families and procreation need to be challenged, and fundamentally new understandings of family need to be developed."[5]

Although there are aspects of both Peters's and Lebacqz's analyses with which I would take issue, they share a central insight that seems to me exactly right: it is the moral character of human relationships within the family, rather than simply the mechanics of embryo generation or the raw biochemistry of genetic identity, that

---

4. Ted Peters, "Cloning Shock: A Theological Reaction," in Ronald Cole-Turner, editor, *Human Cloning: Religious Responses*, (Louisville, Ky.:Westminster John Knox Press), 23.

5. Karen Lebacqz, "Genes, Justice, and Clones," in Cole-Turner, *Human Cloning*, 55-56.

is the heart of the matter. Even the most sensitive analysis of the dignity of procreation as a natural process, or the respect to be accorded the human embryo as an individual entity, will leave something crucial out of the picture, namely, the social practice of parenting as a central human activity. This returns me to the matters with which I began, with the implications of reproductive cloning for how we think about family life, and how we understand and protect the bearing and rearing of children as a moral practice.

WELCOMING THE STRANGER: CONTINGENCY, UNCERTAINTY, AND THE VIRTUES OF PARENTING

In trying to think morally about a possibility for which there is no precedent, it sometimes helps to think carefully about the familiar pattern it proposes to replace. This can be surprisingly difficult to do, for the same familiarity that makes us comfortable also makes us blind to important features of our ordinary experience. This makes it necessary to say some very obvious things about the experience of becoming a parent.

Ian Wilmut, Dolly's scientific progenitor, speaks of people having children in what he calls "the ordinary, fun way." The truth is, it **is** fun; not just the lovemaking, but pregnancy itself. Despite its many discomforts, pregnancy is a perennial wonder, as the child within makes its presence more and more known and felt, as the curiosity and anticipation grow, and parents ponder a thousand variations on the question, "I wonder who it will be?" For the fact is, we don't know. However often we go for ultrasounds, however much we submit to prenatal testing to learn about the gender and size and health of our soon-to-be offspring, even those who embark upon parenting in the most considered and controlled and rational way possible *do not know who is coming.* Having a child is, arguably, the deepest and most enduring connection of which we are capable, and we don't know who it is we are proposing to devote our work and worry to for the next eighteen or twenty years. This has to be the ultimate blind date! Only it is more like an arranged marriage, for when this stranger arrives you are not just courting: you are already committed. If it were not so commonplace, we would think it was madness.

Here is a social arrangement in which rational, self-sufficient actors, perfectly capable of judging their own best interests and maximizing them, commit themselves sight unseen to a being who will reliably cost them enormous time, money, labor, anxiety, and grief for a mixed and unreliable long-range return. Sometimes we do it by conscious choice, carefully timing a pregnancy to fit in with other life activities. Often enough we do it by accident or by default, or for reasons that may be good or bad or foolish. But however it comes about, with an amazing degree of regularity, we accept our children as they come to us, receive them for no other reason than that they somehow belong to us and we to them, and we do our best through the years that follow to figure out what is good for them and provide it as well as we can.

Of course, we do not merely passively receive our children, but also actively shape who they will become, socializing and educating them, forming and directing their development according to our own judgments and convictions. Along with devotion to our children in the present go plans and dreams about their future, and all the goods we hope to see realized in their lives. But no one with any real involvement in the upbringing of a child could subscribe to Locke's theory that a child is a blank tablet upon which anything at all can be written. Children from birth both absorb and resist our influence, bringing to the equation their own inclinations and abilities, their own preferences and limitations, their own nature, and, very soon, their own choices about who they wish to become. The actual experience of parenting is always an interplay between planning and happenstance, between the weighty sense of responsibility and the frustration of helplessness. Experienced parents know they cannot, and wise parents know they should not, undertake to impose their own version of the ideal child upon their offspring. And they also know something of the grief that goes with accepting all the things they care passionately about but cannot control.

What all this underscores is the complexity and delicacy of the moral task that parents undertake, to be thoroughly interested and invested participants in the nurture of another human being who will in the end meet them as an equal, and will certainly not always please them. Parenting is the risky enterprise in which one merely human being sets out to form another, and it requires a whole panoply of virtues: flexibility and courage and humility, humor and restraint and above all a deep generosity of spirit. For here human beings are asked to use an enormous disparity of power unselfishly and with a deliberate intent to see it overturned in the end in favor of the liberty and responsibility of one who stands in primary relation to God. We discover our children's good rather than determine it, and in the end we will complete our duties to our children by stepping back from their lives as they become in actuality what they have always been in origin and in destiny: our peers and not our subjects, fellow creatures with us and "coheirs of the grace of life."

CLONING AS A TECHNIQUE OF SELECTION

On this specifically theological note I want to pause, to propose that we think about what difference it will make to us and to our children if we move from this basic stance of receiving and welcoming and cherishing the children who are born to us to one of selecting them, or more properly selecting in advance a template that is to be reproduced in them. What will it mean to our understanding of our offspring and our relation to them if they are not gifts who surprise us but projects we have engineered, whose most basic biological attributes are the product of our will? What will it do to parenting if we go to such lengths as asexual replication in order to exercise control over every element of the individual genome?

One of the things such a practice will do is to place parental desires, not simply the general desire to have a baby but the desire for a *particular* baby, squarely in the center of what constitutes the parent-child relationship. We will have moved from the experience at once routine and extraordinary of being presented with a child who is one's to nurture and to celebrate, to the quite different experience of the delivery of a specific and intended result, inevitably measured against the prototype chosen for replication. It is not hard to see why so many fear that our attitude about this relationship among both technicians and prospective parents will shift toward child-as-commodity afforded to parent-as-consumer. The traditional language of Christians and Jews, that children are gifts of God, can only seem quaint and out of place in a context in which people can speak without blushing of "quality control."

On the other hand, what cloning will not do is successfully eliminate uncertainty. Some of the rationales proposed for human cloning reflect not only an unseemly desire to control who our offspring will be but also a great lack of sophistication in understanding human development. Any behavioral scientist can tell you that a person is far too complex an interaction of genotype, physical environment, social context, and individual life experience to be engineered reliably. The odds are overwhelming that you cannot make yourself another Michael Jordan or another Yo-Yo Ma, or even another you, even if it were morally legitimate to set out to do so. But the fact that it will not work is little comfort, for what would it be like to live as a failed copy or to be the parent of one? Successful or not, our readiness to engineer the genome of our offspring to obtain a desirable result expresses a lack of fundamental respect for the otherness of our children, who not only are not us but are finally not ours.

In my judgment, human reproductive cloning as a technique of genetic engineering represents a basic distortion of parenting. It displays a failure of the reticence rooted in religious awe with which people of faith should approach intervention in the being of another human creature. This reticence is most important precisely where it is most in danger of subversion, in the intense and emotion-laden relationship between parent and child, where such enormous influence is exerted and such disparate power is exercised. By making our offspring the product not of our bodies and our relationships but of our will, we give a new and peculiarly intimate form to a most fundamental human corruption: the readiness to make ourselves each the center of our own universe and to regard all others in relation to ourselves.

CLONING AS A REMEDY FOR DEPRIVATION

Now finally I come around to the arguments for reproductive cloning as a means of providing a child under special circumstances that rule out other methods. Rationales have included the desire to produce a child who is genetically related to a sterile donor, as in Tendler's example; the wish to replace a dead fetus or child in cases like that proposed by Cole-Turner; and the possibility of providing a genetically related child to a lesbian couple, in Lebacqz's discussion. I will not pretend that such circumstances do not represent real losses, even in some cases real tragedies. But I question whether it is always possible to offer a technical solution to a human reality such as sterility or premature death, and whether it is always desirable to do so simply because it is possible. Such questions are always subject to the charge of heartlessness, especially when they are raised by people who do not confront in their own lives the realities with which these proposals try to grapple. Nevertheless, I think we are in danger of serious distortions of life and thought if we do not think long and hard about what we are trying to do with biomedical technology and why, and if we don't stop to consider who we turn ourselves and each other into along the way. Taking these examples as instances of a larger class of exceptional cases, I will treat them in the order given. My aim is to achieve some clarity about what possibilities cloning would or would not offer in such cases.

Rabbi Tendler's scenario proposes to use cloning to continue a family line for a sterile man whose relatives have all died in the Holocaust. He speaks of a religious and cultural value placed on familial continuity, and of the peculiar horror of the Nazi genocide as destroying whole families, root and branch. These are matters of enormous weight and seriousness, not to be passed off lightly. What the world has lost in the destruction of so much of European Jewry is incalculable, as indeed are the losses of every such slaughter, both those known and those buried in the silence of history. But it is important to be clear about what cloning can and cannot offer here. It cannot restore either the children who were or the children who would have been, not as individuals and not as collective carriers of all the particular genetic mix that might be thought to underlie a "family line." It cannot even give the hypothetical man a child in the normal sense of the word, a descendant half of whose genetic complement comes from the father without replicating any of his genome. It can only give the sterile man a delayed genetic twin, a child who, far from rescuing familial continuity, is not exactly anyone's son or daughter. The idea that this is the only or the best way to resist the destruction of a family strikes me as wrongheaded, as if the transmission of DNA decisively constituted human identity and belonging, and gave meaning to what we express when we call our

families "ours." It seems to me that Rabbi Tendler's hypothetical sur-
vivor would be better served by adopting a child and raising her or
him in the history and the traditions, the memories and the love that
are the real stuff of family life and continuity.

The case envisioned by Cole-Turner is at once more poignant
and more troubling. It presents us with a grief more imaginable and
distinct: the loss of a child late in pregnancy by a couple who can
conceive no more. There is no issue here of genetic replication of
parent or living donor, and no actual developed human being who
would have been selected in the person of the clone. What there is
instead is a chance to cheat death by cloning the fetus from salvaged
tissue, and thus to replace for the couple what, one might argue,
nature and even God intended: a living child born of their union. It
seems we have here the opportunity to provide a technical fix for
tragedy. But do we? Even if we do, is it one we ought to use?

The reality is that such a couple has experienced a real loss, an
actual death, and that fact must not be denied or minimized lest it
come back to haunt both the parents and any child to be born.
Neither by cloning nor by any other technique is it possible to give
back the dead child; the question is whether we ought to try to give
the grieving parents a twin to replace it. In more ordinary circumstances, parents experiencing such a late-term loss would be coun-
seled to take time to live with and come to terms with their grief
before making an effort to conceive a "new" baby, precisely because
of the moral and psychological problems inherent in trying to
replace one human being with another. Such concerns could only be
dramatically heightened if the new fetus were a clone of the child
now dead. As harsh as it may seem, I am convinced that this utterly
understandable impulse is a temptation we should resist. Rather
than finding a technical circumvention of mortality, we must find
the courage to face it squarely, to endure the suffering it imposes,
and to move toward the recovery of faith and hope through grief
rather than around it. As human beings, our task is not to outwit
death, but to become people who can live mortal lives, loving other
mortals wisely and well. Since the natural conception of another
child is (hypothetically) impossible, the alternatives for such a couple would be other means of assisted reproduction (the specific
means would depend on the nature of the infertility, now unspeci-

fied), or the adoption of a child who would be their second child, not a recreation of the first; a child made theirs by love and the thousand shared tasks of parenting, rather than by genetic relationship.

Finally, I turn to the question of whether cloning should be used to extend the right to a child related to them and no one else to couples who in the nature of the case cannot conceive one in the ordinary fashion: lesbian couples. Here I want to affirm Lebacqz's insight that to pose the question in this way reveals how far, and how far astray, we have come in our pursuit of technological reproduction. In our urgency to provide would-be parents with whatever they want, and can pay for, we have allowed ourselves to forget a lesson that should have been burned into our brains with the abolition of slavery and the repeal of laws that made women and children property: no one can have a right to another human being.

In our lives as members of families, however constituted, we are gifted with one another rather than entitled to one another. In living and loving, in giving birth and nurture and care to the next generation, we are charged with the stewardship of the gift of life that we rightly call holy, which at root means simply "belonging to God." We do have responsibilities to one another, and claims not to have our liberty in fulfilling those responsibilities arbitrarily restricted. But none of this amounts to the right to a child, however conceived. A child comes always from beyond us and is oriented beyond us ultimately to the friendship with God for which human beings are made. If we belong to one another, we do so by our devotion to one another's well-being in all its dimensions, by our wisdom about it as well as our commitment to it. Our children are ours, or perhaps more deeply we are theirs, because we receive and welcome them, because we put ourselves in service to them, and finally because we understand both the depth and the limits of human belonging. Our insistence on "children of our own" and our readiness to go to any expense, any risk, any length to obtain offspring who carry our genes and no one else's, reveal not so much our prizing of family as our misunderstanding of it.

10

A Parallel to the Care Given the Soul: An Orthodox View of Cloning and Related Technologies

Rev. Demetri Demopulos, Ph.D.

Father Demetri Demopulos, who is an Orthodox priest with a Ph.D. in genetics, lifts up key principles of Orthodox Christianity—that human beings are destined to grow into the image of God and that medicine is God's gift for our benefit as long as it is applied as a "parallel to the care given the soul." By returning to these ancient principles, Demopulos reframes the debate about cloning and genetic medicine in foundational theological terms. Considered theologically, who we are and why we are here? What new technologies can be used in a way that is consistent with the care of our souls? Warning that we must not do "irreparable harm to our souls as we attempt to heal our bodies," Demopulos cautions us especially about cloning as "the ultimate expression of self-love."

The past several years have seen incredible advances in genetics and embryology. Progress in embryology and cell biology has brought us Dolly, the first mammal cloned from adult, differentiated cells. Since Dolly, many different mammals have been cloned, and some have been genetically modified to produce desired gene products. The Human Genome Project is completing the mapping and sequence of the entire human genome. This will enable scientists to find and characterize genes that may play roles in determining how we look, how well we think, and whether we will be afflicted with a genetic disease. These same breakthroughs in human research have given us the ability to manipulate human embryonic stem cells so that they have the potential to become any cell in our bodies and present the promise of treating life-threatening diseases and organ failures.

As I consider the recent work done in reproductive biology and genetics and speculate on what advances the twenty-first century will bring, I begin my response with the words of a fourth-century theologian and bishop, St. Basil the Great of Caesarea:

> In as much as our body is susceptible to various hurts, . . . and since the body suffers affliction from both excess and deficiency, the medical art has been vouchsafed us by God, who directs our whole life, as a model for the cure of the soul, to guide us in the removal of what is superfluous and in the addition of what is lacking. . . . Consequently, we must take great care to employ this medical art, if it should be necessary, not as making it wholly accountable for our state of health or illness, but as redounding to the glory of God and as a parallel to the care given the soul.[1]

I take the fourth century as my starting point, not because I am more comfortable there, nor because the Greek Orthodox Church is unable or unwilling to deal with contemporary issues, but because the response of any Orthodox Christian clergyman or theologian should be well grounded in the Tradition of the Orthodox Church. This Tradition is the compilation of those things that the church, as the body of Christ, has given us to help us find the way to God. It includes Holy Scripture, the canons of the church, the pronouncements of the ecumenical councils, the divine liturgies, and patristic texts, and we look to it for guidance when faced with new challenges. Although ancient, it is a living Tradition that speaks to modern concerns as well as it spoke to those in the past.

I cannot turn to a patristic text to find a statement on the cloning either of humans or other mammals. I will not encounter explicit references to stem cell research anywhere in our patristic tradition. What will be clear, however, is the basic understanding of what it is to be human and what our relationship to God is. I can therefore extrapolate from the writings of the fathers the "mind of the church" in response to these issues.

---

1. St. Basil the Great, *The Long Rules*, 55, translated by M.M. Wagner; *St. Basil: Ascetical Works*, volume 9, *The Fathers of the Church*, (Washington, D.C.: Catholic University of America Press, 1962), 330-332.

My discussion of cloning, stem cell therapy, and modification of the human genome will be based on this patristic understanding of who we are and what we are doing here. I began with a quotation from St. Basil because he provided a standard by which cloning and genetic advances can be measured. Basil's *The Long Rules* was written to answer a series of questions from a monastic brotherhood. The quotation above is part of the reply to the final question: "whether recourse to the medical art is in keeping with the practice of piety."[2] In responding to this question, Basil acknowledged the need to use medicine, science, and technology to treat disease. He proclaimed these tools to be gifts from God to enable us to heal ourselves. He cautioned, however, against the tendency to misuse them and against our proclivity to place our inventions at the center of our concerns. The practice of medicine is a tool to alleviate suffering and treat disease, not an end in itself. His insistence that therapeutic treatment of disease parallel the treatment of the soul shows us the limitations we should place on new technologies.

To explain these limits, we need to explore first what it is to be human. Orthodox Christian Tradition holds that God created human beings in his image and likeness.[3] It teaches that humans are unique in creation because we alone are both spiritual and physical beings, body and soul at the same time, in a mysterious manner akin to the theanthropic Christ who is at the same time God and man. As psychosomatic beings, humans are called to grow and develop in relationship with God and each other until we are granted the gift of theosis, or deification, "and become partakers of the divine nature."[4] By struggling to attain theosis we can also fulfill the will of God that all things be united in him through Christ. "For he has made known to us in all wisdom and insight the mystery of his will, according to his purpose which he set forth in Christ as a plan for the fulness of time, to unite all things in him, things in heaven and things on earth."[5] Humans, then, are called to bring all things together in

---

2. St. Basil the Great, *The Long Rules*, 330.
3. Gen 1:26; all scripture quotations are from the Revised Standard Version.
4. 2 Pet 1:4.
5. Eph 1:9-10.

Christ. We are asked to act as priests of creation to offer back to God the things that he has given us, thus allowing for and facilitating the sanctification of creation and the unity of all things in Christ.[6]

Finally, I want to distinguish between the Orthodox understanding of human being and human person. The human being is the creature who is called to do the things mentioned above, the one who is in the image of God. The authentic human person, however, is one who has achieved the goal God has set for us, has grown in the image, and reached the likeness of God. The authentic human person is one who is deified, who has achieved theosis.[7] Those of us who are still struggling toward theosis are human beings but potential human persons. Our Tradition also maintains that the process of growth toward theosis begins at conception. Embryos, fetuses, infants, children, and adults are all potential human persons growing in the image of God toward his likeness. Each must be given the respect and dignity due every authentic person because it is God's will that all people become authentic persons, in union with him.

These beliefs are the bases for the Orthodox Church's long and consistent stand against abortion and any procedure that sacrifices the viability of any potential human person. St. Basil the Great equates abortion with murder of an embryo regardless of whether it was "formed" or "unformed."[8] He did not maintain a developmental threshold for determining personhood; even an embryo that did not yet look human was to be protected. Today we know more about reproduction and can say that the human zygote is genetically and

---

6. See also Panayiotis Nellas, *Deification in Christ: The Nature of the Human Person* (Crestwood, N.Y.: St. Vladimir's Seminary Press, 1987), chapters 1 and 2; John Breck, *The Sacred Gift of Life: Orthodox Christianity and Bioethics* (Crestwood, N.Y.: St. Vladimir's Seminary Press, 1998), chapters 1 and 3; and John D. Zizioulas, "Preserving God's Creation: Lecture Three," *King's College Theological Review,* 13(1990): 1-5.

7. John D. Zizioulas, *Being as Communion: Studies in Personhood and the Church* (Crestwood, N.Y.: St. Vladimir's Seminary Press, 1985), 49-56.

8. St. Basil the Great, "To Amphilochius, concerning the Canons," Letter 188, in *Nicene and Post-Nicene Fathers,* Second Series, volume 8, edited by P. Schaff and H. Wace. (Grand Rapids, Mich.: Wm. B. Eerdmans, 1983), 223-228.

developmentally committed to becoming a human being. As such, it is our responsibility to nurture and protect it so that it has every chance to grow and develop in fulfillment of God's will.

REPRODUCTIVE CLONING

The prospect of cloning a human being is technically remote but theoretically real. The requirements in donor cells and eggs for nuclear transfer into enucleated oocytes[9] are great, and it is difficult to imagine a group able to finance the necessary research in humans or accumulate the required oocytes. Even if feasible economically, the cost in lost embryos because of failed attempts would be sufficient for the Orthodox to oppose it. What would we say, however, if the procedure were perfected and a clone could be made without any more risk of failure than a natural pregnancy? To answer this, I apply the limits St. Basil established and ask two questions. Is it therapeutic, and does it parallel the care of the soul?

To be therapeutic, a procedure has to bring about an improved condition, whether restoration to complete health or alleviation of symptoms. If cloning were used as a form of reproduction, what condition would it then be treating? It would not be the emotional suffering of parents who cloned a lost child, because the clone would not be that child. After all, clones would be twins displaced in time. As we know, twins may look alike, but they are distinct and different people. It is impossible to recover a person by cloning; the best we can do is to perpetuate a genome.

Perhaps cloning could be used to correct infertility in couples. Nuclear transfer technology would assure that the child would be related to one of the infertile parents. Perhaps two children could be cloned, a boy and a girl, each derived from one of the "parents." This assumes that infertility is a disease or condition requiring cure or correction, a position I reject. The problem is not infertility but childlessness. Childlessness is more easily treated through adoption than is infertility through in vitro fertilization techniques or cloning.

---

9. I. Wilmut, A.E. Schnieke, J. McWhir, A.J. Kind, and K.H.S. Campbell, "Viable Offspring Derived from Fetal and Adult Mammalian Cells," *Nature*, 385 (1997), 810–813.

Some will argue that infertility is indeed a condition that needs treatment. The inability to bring one's own biological offspring into the world can be debilitating to some couples, and the only cure is to give them recourse to technologically assisted procreation. Some individuals' sense of worth is closely connected to the ability to reproduce, and this needs therapeutic intervention. I do not deny that nor that cloning to overcome infertility can be *therapeutic* in some cases.

Even so, I still do not think it should be done, because reproductive cloning ultimately falls outside the limits established for the medical arts to parallel the care of the soul. Care of the soul means practicing whatever discipline is necessary to reach the goal God has set for us—union with him. We humans have a propensity to follow our own will and disregard the will of others, all others, including God. In the Orthodox Tradition this is called self-love. By succumbing to it we draw away from God and from one another. We create divisions and distinctions although God wills that all things be united in Him. By distancing ourselves from God in this way, we fall into sin, and the farther away we move, the harder it is to return through repentance. Proper care of the soul is that which helps us overcome self-love and move nearer to God, and cloning is not proper care.

To create a child that is genetically identical to oneself strikes me as the ultimate expression of self-love. It denies how the Orthodox Church views procreation. A child is ideally the product of the expression of love between a husband and wife. As a result of that love, and through the grace of God, a child is conceived, develops, and grows in the image and likeness of God as a unique individual containing equal parts of the parents. Cloning prohibits the manifestation of the couple's love and unity of the couple by eliminating the child's shared genetic composition. The child becomes a possession rather than a creation, and its humanity is thus diminished. Division and distinction are promoted, and divinely willed unity is lost. Cloning clearly cannot be considered proper care for the soul. I believe it would be better to help those suffering from infertility to look outward toward others and toward God. We need to expend the energy needed to combat a society that often teaches selfishness as a virtue and that has adopted a materialism which allows personal value to be measured only through possessions and offspring. The churches must play a role in redirecting people's focus away from themselves and toward God. Then perhaps we may be able to disregard infertility and cure childlessness by caring for the orphaned and abandoned children in the world.

STEM CELLS AND THERAPEUTIC CLONING

The isolation and culture of human embryonic stem cells[10] have provided previously unknown potential for treatment of human disease. Pluripotent cells that can differentiate into any number of cell types may play an important role in treating neurological disorders, aiding burn victims with skin grafts, and treating organ failure. The possibility of improving human life is great. Embryonic stem cells, however, are isolated from sacrificed embryos in the blastocyst stage, and termination of human life at any stage of development is immoral according to the Orthodox Church. How do we resolve this problem? Do we go forward with stem cell research because of its potential therapeutic good, or do we oppose it because it destroys potential human beings?

Much has been written about the ethics of human embryonic stem cell research. The National Bioethics Advisory Commission has released a report recommending that federal funding of embryonic stem cell research be allowed if the cells are derived from "cadaveric fetal tissue and embryos remaining after infertility treatments."[11] The Ethics Advisory Board of the Geron Corporation, which funded the initial isolation of embryonic stem cells, presented a detailed and careful evaluation of the ethical and moral issues in using embryos as a source of stem cells.[12] The conclusions of both of these reports, and numerous others,[13] are that

---

10. J. A. Thomson, J. Itskovitz-Eldor, S. S. Shapiro, M. A. Waknitz, J. J. Swiergiel, V. S. Marshall, and J. M. Jones, "Embryonic Stem Cell Lines Derived from Human Blastocysts," *Science,* 282 (1998): 1145-1147.

11. National Bioethics Advisory Commission, *Ethical Issues in Human Stem Cell Research,* volume 1: *Report and Recommendations of the National Bioethics Advisory Commission* (Rockville, Md.: 1999), 68.

12. Geron Ethics Advisory Board, "Research with Human Embryonic Stem Cells: Ethical Considerations," *Hastings Center Report,* 29 (1999): 31-36.

13. For recent reviews and viewpoints, see the special issue, "Stem Cell Research and Ethics," *Science,* 287 (2000): 1417-1446.

the benefits to humanity from stem cells outweigh any moral constraints over the use of blastocysts to obtain them.

Cloning technology and stem cell isolation could be combined to perfect a method of providing autologous cells for cell replacement therapy or for tissue transplantation to repair damaged organs. Histocompatibility and rejection problems would be eliminated if replacement cells or organs were obtained from stem cells derived from the patient through nuclear transfer cloning.[14] The somatic cells would be cloned just as Dolly was, but instead of allowing the clone to develop and be born, as in reproductive cloning, it would be sacrificed at the blastocyst stage to harvest the stem cells. The cells would then be processed to differentiate into the desired cell type for treatment.

Therapeutic cloning does not present the problems that accompany reproductive cloning regarding distinctions between cloned and "natural" individuals or motivations for cloning. The therapeutic clones would never reach maturity. The sole purpose of their generation would be to treat illness and save lives. The clone would, however, go through an initial stage of growth and development that commits it to becoming a human being, a potential human person, and we cannot condone the destruction of a potential human person, no matter what the stage of development.

The good resulting from stem cell therapy is too great to abandon it. Instead, we should urge research to develop stem cells from morally acceptable donors. Recent reports indicate that adult stem cells may be less restricted than previously thought and that stem cells that normally produce tissue-specific cell types could, when transplanted, produce different cell types. For example, murine neural stem cells that normally produce only brain cells were shown to produce blood cells and hematopoietic cells in bone-marrow-depleted mice.[15] The use of such adult stem cells could provide the therapy envisioned in

---

14. See Kenneth W. Culver, Chapter 2, this volume.

15. R.R. Christopher, Rodney L. Bjornson, Brent A. Rietze, M. Reynolds, Cristina Magli, and Angelo L. Vesconi, "Turning Brain into Blood: A Hematopoietic Fate Adopted by Adult Neural Stem Cells in Vivo," *Science,* 283 (1999): 534-537; see also Irving L. Weissman, "Translating Stem and Progenitor Cell Biology to the Clinic: Barriers and Opportunities," *Science,* 287 (2000): 1442-1446.

the use of embryonic cell lines without the need to sacrifice the donor. This would remove my objections to stem cell therapy. The research on and application of adult stem cells would be therapeutic to the body and would parallel the proper care of the soul. No distinctions between potential human persons would be necessary, and unity in the course of therapy would be promoted. This fits the criteria St. Basil established to be pleasing to God.

CLONING AND GENOME MANIPULATION

The ability to transfer genes by recombinant DNA technology and create transgenic animals has enormous therapeutic potential. Introducing human genes into animals and selecting those that properly express them could provide us with efficient, inexpensive sources of proteins, hormones, and other biochemicals that are useful in treatment of disease. Cloning technology can greatly aid the establishment of these transgenic stocks.

Traditional methods of increasing the number of transgenic animals and establishing breeding stocks are cumbersome and time-consuming. Animals must be bred and progeny screened for the desired trait. Selected animals are then interbred and their progeny screened again until sufficient generations have elapsed to ensure that all progeny properly express the trait and that sufficient numbers of transgenic animals exist for harvest. Cloning could drastically reduce the time and labor involved in producing transgenic stocks. A single transgenic animal could be cloned any number of times[16] to establish a primary breeding stock or increase numbers for production. Screening subsequent generations and cloning improved transgenic animals could easily and quickly provide relief for people afflicted with insulin-dependent diabetes, hemophilia, or other illnesses that result from an inability to synthesize a protein or metabolite.

I support this sort of cloning and genome manipulation. The therapeutic potential for pharmaceuticals could substantially reduce

---

16. Y. Kato, T. Tani, Y. Sotomaru, K. Kurokawa, J. Kato, H. Doguchi, H. Yasue, and Y. Tsunoda, "Eight Calves Cloned from Somatic Cells of a Single Adult," *Science*, 282 (1998): 2095-2098.

illness and suffering in the world, and this concern for the welfare of others brings us closer to each other and to God. The animals, as well, would not be treated in any substantially different way than domesticated animals are now, and I do not object to the cultivation of domesticated animals.

I am uneasy, however, because I am unsure of the motives of the commercial concerns involved in this research. I fear that the primary motivation for pharmaceutical companies is simply and exclusively the pursuit of profit. The arguments industry offers in defense of patent rights for DNA sequences are the need to protect investors and ensure a profit. I am not convinced that companies engaged in therapeutic cloning of transgenic animals, should this prove profitable, will refrain from selling gene products to enhance people able to pay for them. Furthermore, what would prevent them from applying transgenic techniques to humans to modify their genomes?

The completion of the Human Genome Project will provide a great deal of information on the human condition. There will eventually be a catalog of genes known to govern expression of various traits. Some of these lead to debilitating, lethal genetic diseases; others are responsible for normal variation within our human population. Attempts are being made today to treat genetic disorders with somatic gene therapy, where conditions are corrected *in situ* by modification of the somatic genome. At the present time, however, it is easier genetically to modify embryos before the soma and germline diverge, thus making the modification heritable.[17] Instead of making transgenic animals that carry beneficial human genes, modified humans will have the genes in their own bodies and pass them on to their offspring.

Somatic gene therapy poses no moral or ethical problem when used to relieve diseases that brutalize and shorten human life. Providing afflicted individuals with a better chance to grow physically and spiritually, thus growing closer to God, is central to the concept of therapy and proper care for the soul, but correcting natural variation to conform to a societal norm is not. The former leads to unity in God; the latter promotes cosmetic conformity and

17. Jon W. Gordon, "Genetic Enhancement in Humans," *Science,* 283 (1999): 2023-2024.

establishes distinctions and divisions among people. As St. Paul told the Romans, "For as in one body we have many members, and all the members do not have the same function, so we, though many, are one body in Christ, and individually members one of another."[18] He did not tell them to be exactly the same.

The Orthodox Christian understands that we are all defective in some respect. Our challenge is to overcome and transcend our deficiencies as we progress toward union with God. We also have a natural tendency to want to eliminate adversity, pain, and suffering. It would be easy to look to genome modification in embryos as a way to correct serious defects in our genetic makeup, but I am not sure that would be a good thing. The Orthodox stance on sanctity of life from the zygote leads me to oppose gene-modification trials in human embryos if they require sacrificing them, but I will not limit my opposition to safety issues.[19] If I argue against something because it is unsafe, I would have no argument if it became safe, and I am opposed to germ line genome modification because it divides us and separates us from God.

Germ line modification, even if used only for genetic lethal conditions, will create a class of people distinct from others. As more people are relieved of their genetic afflictions, more will want the standards of permission to be lowered to include nonlethal conditions. This will lead us to provide genetic enhancement to anyone who can afford it, thus reducing our humanity to a mere commodity. Instead of uniting us in our knowledge that each of us must transcend some disability and working to improve imperfect lives for all, we will divide ourselves into any number of categories and struggle with the impossible task of creating perfect lives for some.

Ted Peters provides an excellent overview of arguments for and against germ line intervention and modification.[20] He favors at least keeping an open mind toward their application and leans decidedly in favor of using them to alleviate suffering and eliminating disease.

18. Romans 12:4-5.

19. See Gordon, "Genetic Enhancement in Humans," for a good, brief discussion of safety issues concerning genome modification.

20. Ted Peters, *Playing God? Genetic Determinism and Human Freedom* (New York: Routledge, 1997), 143-156.

His theological and ethical justification is the concept of humanity as "created co-creator," developed by Philip Hefner:

> Human beings are God's created co-creators whose purpose is to be the agency, acting in freedom, to birth the future that is most wholesome for the nature that has birthed us—the nature that is not only our own genetic heritage, but also the entire human community and the evolutionary and ecological reality in which and to which we belong. Exercising this agency is said to be God's will for humans.[21]

In my view, this is an over optimistic and narrow understanding of humanity's role in creation that can be and has been used to justify many actions that greatly damaged creation and jeopardized our future existence. Our creative investigations into the physical structure of matter led to the healing use of nuclear medicine but also to the development and use of nuclear weapons. It establishes a divine purpose for our creativity: if we are created to create, then anything we create is the will of God.

The Tower of Babel story tells of a great act of human imagination and industry that resulted in further divisions among humanity, not because humanity was creative and built a great tower, but because the tower was built to fulfill purely human goals. When humanity believes that it can replace God, all creation is in trouble, and the created co-creator model can too easily give way to this. I cannot think of a more apt modern-day Tower of Babel than the idea of modifying humanity to fit a human ideal of what it is to be human.

The "priest of creation" concept offered by John Zizioulas takes as its model the Incarnate God and Archpriest, Jesus Christ.[22] As we are called to follow Christ, we are asked to emulate his sacrificial love for the whole world, not just the people inhabiting it, but the world itself. During each Orthodox eucharistic celebration, the priest raises the bread and wine and says, "We offer to You these gifts from Your own gifts in all and for all." It is important that the gifts being offered, bread and wine, are products of

---

21. Philip Hefner, *The Human Factor: Evolution, Culture, Religion* (Philadelphia: Fortress Press, 1993), 27.
22. Zizioulas, "Preserving God's Creation."

human creativity and industry; they do not occur in nature. Clearly, humanity must create in order to offer gifts to God. The critical point, however, is that we create in order to offer to God, not simply for our own use. When we create to offer to God, we may be more likely to think twice about what we are creating so that it will be an offering pleasing to God.

Nothing we do is as critical as what we do to ourselves. We need to take great care to ensure that we do not do irreparable harm to our souls as we attempt to heal our bodies, that we do not build Towers of Babel, but instead provide proper offerings to our Creator.

11

Toward a Theology
for the Age of Biotechnology

Ronald Cole-Turner

As things are, there is no reason to assume that anything we might reasonably conceive of doing with living tissues might not be possible; living tissues are proving to be remarkably compliant. . . . [W]e can look forward to an age in which the understanding of life's mechanisms will be virtually total, that is, the principal systems will be understood molecule by molecule. From this total understanding will come—if we choose—total control. Of course the word "total" is too absolute. There will always be deficiencies and inconsistencies. Biology will never come to an end. But for practical purposes we might as well assume that absolute control will be possible. It is not irresponsible—nor, indeed, sensationalist—to suggest this. It is irresponsible to imply the opposite, that our power will always be too limited to worry about. We are entering the age of biological control, and we should gird our moral and political loins accordingly.[1]

What are we to think of this "age of biological control," with its promises of unprecedented power to control life through technology? Or should we be asking instead what makes us think we can control this technology, or if anything can?

---

1. Ian Wilmut and Keith Campbell, "The New Biotechnology," in Ian Wilmut, Keith Campbell, and Colin Tudge, *The Second Creation: Dolly and the Age of Biological Control* (New York: Farrar, Straus and Giroux, 2000), 264.

It is difficult enough just to learn how to think about this technology, simply to understand it and to interpret it correctly, without exaggerating its powers or minimizing its significance. Far too many descriptions of biotechnology exaggerate the power of cloning and genetic engineering, sometimes in order to make grand promises about its benefits and to secure public support, sometimes to encourage opposition through warning of the grave dangers of this new technology. But then there are those who minimize the powers of biotechnology, some to oppose it by dismissing its claims and challenging its value as a research investment, others to discourage too much attention or scrutiny. A fair assessment is hard to find.

Claims of "biological control," whether from Ian Wilmut and Keith Campbell or from their critics, are in fact too sweeping. Granted, *bios*—the Greek word for life and the subject matter of biology—is remarkably plastic and complies readily with our wishes. This is the real point in the philosophical rejection of the nineteenth-century idea of vitalism, the view that life itself is a force or hidden power that transcends the mechanisms of the organism. Now philosophers and biologists and almost all biotechnologists agree: there is no mysterious stuff called *life* that is unknowable to science or inaccessible to technology; therefore, there is such a thing as biotechnology.

But we must be precise, and "control of life" and even the word *biotechnology* are anything but precise. These terms are vague, sweeping, and too grand for the limited extent of human control. Genetic engineering and the other technologies that we call biotechnology offer us a little power to control some of the genetic co-determinants of life, but they leave much outside our control, and what is uncontrolled by technology is equally co-determinant of life. We can modify life but not control it. We can nudge it along pathways of our choosing, but we cannot dominate it or rule it, precisely because we cannot control its environmental determinants.

Genetic engineering and biotechnology are sharply limited to the control of certain molecular, genetic, and cellular functions and processes, all of which are merely components of "life" or of the *bios* in biology. True, we have learned to modify DNA, at least with some success. We have learned how to isolate and control cells at the beginning of the differentiation process (stem cells), and we are beginning to learn how to guide their differentiation. We have learned how, at least in some species like sheep, to reprogram DNA from fully differentiated cells so that it begins again as an embryo. These are important but limited powers, and even when their potential is fully realized, they do not add up to control of *life* for the simple reason that life is more than DNA.

Even if we grant that we can have some effect upon the environment surrounding an organism, or upon the exposure of an individual to its environment, we still must see an absolute limit that confronts our technology. Power to modify genes will control life only to the extent that genes themselves control life, and that is a limited extent. As our technology improves, we will gain greater power to control genes, but we will always face the limit that exists in nature itself. The environment as a whole is almost entirely beyond control, and to an overwhelming extent it always will be. Our point of access to life's plasticity is limited to our powers of genetic control. Because genes are not all-powerful, genetic engineering will never be all-controlling. And on a grander scale, that of ecosystems and species over eons, our efforts to "control evolution" will always be limited by nature or the environment, which forever exerts its selective pressure upon our creations.

To say we "control life" is therefore an exaggeration, but to say we have no significant power over life is equally inaccurate and irresponsible. Even in view of all these limits, some having to do with the early state of our technology, others more permanently grounded in the limited significance of genes, it is nevertheless true that the technologies of the present, and surely those of the foreseeable future, put within our hands an unprecedented power over life, if not to control it directly and completely, then at least to modify and steer it toward our ends. Genes may not be all-powerful, but they are at least co-determinant, and if we can modify them, we can leverage their power. That is power enough over life and over nature, perhaps even too much power for any one species to possess.

And we are only beginning. We have a rough draft of the genome, but we know almost nothing of what it means. Learning what the sequence means will be far more difficult than finding it in the first place. But we will soon learn how genes interact with each other and how the genome functions as a whole, and in time we will gain a fuller understanding of how our modifications may affect outcomes in what would seem now to be surprising ways. Today our powers are limited and our techniques lack precision and comprehensiveness, but many of these limits will be cast aside whether by slow, painstaking work or by surprising leaps. It is dangerous to overestimate our wisdom or underestimate our ingenuity.

This power has come quickly. In a single generation, biology has been transformed from a science to a technology, even to a business. Until the early 1970s, biologists were largely limited to watching cells and organisms develop, as if life were a movie that could only be watched. Now biologists have become bio*techno*logists, with technology quite literally inserted into the center of a scientific discipline of observation, and biotechnologists have begun to put their fingers on the movie's rewind button and on its fast-forward button. Cloning, the rewind button, lets biotechnologists make nuclear DNA dedifferentiate, sending it back to its developmental beginning and making it start the differentiation process all over again. Stem cells offer the fast-forward button, and with it biotechnology can guide cell differentiation forward quickly along controlled developmental pathways.

We are no longer merely watching life. In a limited but important sense, we are modifying it. With the combined powers of cloning, stem cell technology, gene modification and transfer, and the knowledge that comes from the genome project, we are quickly claiming unprecedented powers. Not only can we move cells backward and forward through their developmental processes; we can, through genetic engineering, edit the genes along the way. Furthermore, through the completion of the Human Genome Project and the publication of the "rough draft" of the entire genome in 2000, we can now begin to understand how the full set of human genes work together so that we can understand the genetic context in which our genetic engineering introduces changes. We can control the fast-forward function (stem cells) and reverse (cloning). We can begin to comprehend how the details in each scene, in each frame of the movie, fit together to make a whole (genomics). And soon we can edit the detail of each scene (genetic engineering), perhaps even before the movie begins (germ line modification).

These powers have their limits, but even with those limits clearly in view, we must see that our power is awesome and that possessing it should be sobering. How shall we control our control? How shall we guide the use of our powers? With this technology in our hands, what future will we create? What visions of the future guide our research, our policies, and our actions? Who is privy to decisions that affect us all, and how is agreement achieved?

It is of course too early to tell exactly where all this will lead. Science fiction offers visions of the genetic future, perhaps the best known of which is the movie *Gattaca*, which suggests that human germ line enhancement will create a privileged class. Lee Silver predicts that if the current rate of technological change remains on course, we will reach a time in about two centuries when our technology begins to have a significant evolutionary impact. "It was a critical turning point in the evolution of life in the universe . . .Throughout it all, there were those who said we couldn't go any further, that there were limits to mental capacity and technological advances. But those prophesied limits were swept aside, one after another, as intelligence, knowledge, and technological power continued to rise." Changes up to that point, in Silver's view, will have produced smarter bioengineers, who are able to take the next step, leading to a period of rapid species change, until, in more than a millennium, "a special point has now been reached in the distant future. And in this era, there exists a special group of mental beings. Although these beings can trace their ancestry back directly to *homo sapiens*, they are as different from humans as humans are from the primitive worms with tiny brains that first crawled along the earth's surface."[2]

The real future, I expect, will be quite tame by comparison. But Silver's fantastic visions raise for us the question of one of the broadest possible contexts of naturalistic meaning of our technology, namely, that of evolutionary biology and the natural history of our species. No species is eternal. We came into existence, and according to everything biology can tell us, we will vanish, with or without a trace. Whether we become more than one species is, of

---

2. Lee M. Silver, *Remaking Eden: How Genetic Engineering and Cloning Will Transform the American Family* (New York: Avon Books, 1997), 292-93.

course, highly doubtful. And if Silver's apocalyptic vision is too dramatic for us, consider the comparatively restrained prose of Ian Wilmut: "As the decades and centuries pass, the science of cloning and the technologies that may flow from it will affect all aspects of human life—the things that people can do, the way we live, even, if we choose, the kinds of people we are."[3] Even when we dismiss the exaggerations and stay to the limits of biotechnology, it is still right and necessary to ask whether biotechnology will *count* for anything in an evolutionary frame of reference. Does it have a place in the natural history of our species and indeed in creating whatever "natural future" may lie ahead for us?

But in a way this is the wrong question, or at least a secondary question. The primary question is theological, and it asks how we refer our technology to God. How do we speak of God and biotechnology in the same sentence? Is there a relationship between what we are doing and what God is doing, so that we can do our work in reference to God's work? If so, then God, not nature, defines the values and purposes of our actions. It is God's future and not evolution against which we measure our acts and assess their audacity and legitimacy. It is God's purposes for our offspring, not our own, that must regulate our use of technology to shape future generations. We and our technology belong to God. All things are from God and to God. All things find their meaning and destiny in relation to God.

So we ask how to assess the *theological* significance of biotechnology. When we ask the question this way, we see that the most immediate concern is not the distant object of our evolutionary fantasies but the present objectification of our nature. We are quickly becoming our own project, and our modification is soon to be a specialized field of our own engineering. In this simple way, human biotechnology fits within and contributes to an essential redefinition of the human person, of relationships between persons, of social structures, and of human destiny. These four themes—persons, relationships, structures, and destiny—have been explored in various ways by the other contributors to this book. Here at the conclusion I want to offer a few summary comments.

---

3. Ian Wilmut, "The Importance of Being Dolly," in Wilmut, Campbell, and Tudge, *The Second Creation*, 5.

When we ask first about the impact of biotechnology upon individual human persons, we see that the first measure of the magnitude of the changes wrought by our technology lies not in the fuzzy horizons of evolution but in its immediate impact on individual selves. For what is most significant at least for now and the coming decade is that we are embracing a wholly new attitude toward ourselves. We are coming to see ourselves not as souls in bodies, not as persons whose freedom and identity are almost entirely independent of our being embodied, but as mere organisms, defined bottom-up by our genes. In our new view of ourselves, mind is the mere experience of the brain. "Soul" is not a separate and inaccessible dimension of humanity but is merely the highest level of our capacities, a level we can touch with technology. We can medicate the self and someday, perhaps, engineer the soul. That we can do so affects how we see ourselves.

Taken to its extreme, this view is reductionistic and dangerously dehumanizing. The human self is seen as nothing but a by-product of its constituent parts, its molecules and genes. Already we can see this shift of attitude, driven by technology and forced upon us as a new metaphysics or more precisely, we should say, a new metatechnology, a truth that follows upon technology. Because we can modify selves, selves must be modifiable, therefore biological and material. Consider the observation of Peter Kramer, the psychiatrist who describes his own conversion from a believer in talk therapy appropriate for transcendent selves to psychopharmacology suited for biological selves: "When one pill at breakfast makes you a new person, or makes your patient, or relative, or neighbor a new person, it is difficult to resist the suggestion, the visceral certainty, that who people are is largely biologically determined."[4]

And if so, tomorrow's genetic approaches offer even greater attractions, greater leverage, and greater control than today's psychopharmacology. Tied to both these technologies is the new metatechnology, the conviction that if we can manipulate the genes, we can manipulate the self. But it is not clear which comes first, the

---

4. Peter D. Kramer, *Listening to Prozac: A Psychiatrist Explores Antidepressant Drugs and the Remaking of the Self* (New York: Viking Penguin, 1993), 18.

technology or the conviction, whether technology drives thought, or vice versa. Surely there will always be the Kramers, the converts, whose views of reality will be changed because technology seems to change reality. But does a changing view lead the way by demanding a new technology to validate itself and to make itself effectual?

It is troubling to have a reductionistic view of human persons grow in popularity just as biotechnology grows in power. The temptation here is that we will embrace the technologies of genetic modification as a solution to our deepest human problems, perhaps even hoping to engineer our own salvation and our own grace. There is good reason to think that we are already using psychopharmacology in this way, to seek molecular cures to spiritual problems. We are coming to see ourselves, at our core or spiritual essence, as biological and manipulable, and we are doing this at the very moment when we are acquiring the biotechnologies of manipulation. Whichever comes first, the technology or the metatechnology, their timing is no mere coincidence.

There is of course a contrasting view of the self that lies at the opposite extreme. It holds that the soul or self is completely different from the biological organism, even to the point of surviving the death of the body. This view, too, is troubling, because those who hold it might be tempted to think that the biological dimension of humanity can be manipulated without any effect whatsoever on the self or the soul. Precisely because the self is beyond manipulation, bioengineering of the human organism is no big deal. The danger here is underestimation.

The truth lies in the middle and in the view that the self is more than genes but is defined by genes. In all respects, the soul or self is dependent upon the molecular level of our biological and organic processes. Our ability to modify the molecular and the genetic is therefore the ability to modify the self. Genetic technology is of course limited to acting upon genes, and, as we have already seen, it is sharply limited in that respect and cannot be seen as "control of life." And here lies an additional limit, for the human self is more than genes, more even than genes plus environment. It is in all its features dependent upon these processes, but as self it emerges from the biological matrix of genes and environment and rises into the realm of the mental, the psychological, the spiritual, into the realm of free and responsible personhood. Technical modifications at the molecular and genetic level can affect some of the preconditions and the predispositions of the mental, moral, and spiritual life, but cannot control it in the details of its behavior or beliefs. Our technology—especially the technology that is to come in the next few decades—is powerful but not all-powerful. It is important here to recognize that the limits of technology's power are established not because the technology is not good but because of the metaphysics of the self as an emergent phenomenon, constrained by but not wholly confined by the molecular and the genetic.

The twofold danger here, to repeat, is reductionism on one side and dualism on the other. Reductionism leads to grand and dangerous illusions about the power of technology to engineer the person by engineering the genome. It promises more control than it can deliver, and it seduces us with that promise. Dualism on the other leads religious people in particular to ignore this technology, to see it as impotent in its claims to affect the core of our personhood and therefore as theologically unimportant. Between these extremes stands the Christian theological tradition of the self as a psychosomatic unity, which is not only correct theology but necessary for a proper assessment of ourselves and our powers. God has created human life as a psychosomatic unity, calling us forth through the processes of mutation and natural selection, gene sequence and gene expression, through processes that we now understand and can modify to some extent. Given that we are created this way, we can in some measure re-create ourselves. That is a fact, or soon will be. The question is how we understand the theological significance of that fact and the moral wisdom that flows from it.

Our wisdom and its absence will be evident in the relationships between people, the second of our themes, and here most poignantly in our relationship as parents to future children who may be brought into existence as a result of genetic modification. The unease that many people have over this prospect might be summarized in this way:

> "Designer children," it may be argued, are engineered, contrivances of the will, artifacts of human action, and *therefore* not human themselves, at least not in respect to the relationship they should

have with parents. Although ever so slightly, the genetic basis of their existence has been compromised in respect to its being free of human artifice. Will subverts being, not because the designer either harms or improves the designed, but because designed and designer cannot be persons in mutual relationship. They are destined forever to be engineer and artifact. A designed child is not a child at all, for being a child implies having a relationship with parents. A designed person is not a person in the fullest sense, for being a person is possible only as person-in-relationship to other persons. The designed person is a product of a technology in the service of a human will that ignores an intrinsic limit imposed by the logic of persons: If I design you, you are to me not a *you* but an *it*.[5]

How do we assess such dis-ease? How do we think about the effect of biotechnology on human relationships from within the framework of God's ordering of the creation and of the relationships among its creatures, including parents and children?

Here we are driven immediately to the language of gift. Children are a gift of God, imperfect, fragile, unpredictable, and yet precious precisely for these reasons. They are an outflow of love, and they are to be loved unconditionally. We are to care for them, and the goal of our caring is to nourish their free and distinct identity so that in time we may come to know them not as parent and child but as our equals in humanity and as our friends. If that is true, then in what ways and how far may technology enter the relationship? May we use technology to alter the genes with which they are born and still relate to them as gifts, as persons? I believe it is possible, but if so it will be because we have attended carefully to all the risks and learned to avoid them.

The use of reproductive cloning is a special concern in this regard. Could a cloned child be a child, a person in mutual relationship? Suppose a young person dies and the parents clone the one they have lost to start a new life. The new child, the clone, would be caught in an awful dilemma: be loved by being like the

5. Ronald Cole-Turner, "Human Limits: Theological Perspectives on Human Germ Line Modification," in Audrey R. Chapman and Mark S. Frankel, editors, *Human Genetic Modifications across Generations: Assessing Scientific, Ethical, Religious, and Policy Issues* (forthcoming).

original and thereby lose your unique identity, or seize upon your uniqueness as a person, not a clone, and thereby reject the reason for your existence. Now, it is possible to imagine a scenario in which the original is not known, and so this argument against cloning, like all the arguments against it, in my opinion, fails to make an absolute and comprehensive case. Nevertheless, the arguments against cloning raise so many concerns, and the arguments for reproductive cloning are so notoriously weak, that on balance we can only oppose it. Someday it will probably become technically or medically safe. But it will never be possible, except by many experiments over decades, to say that it is psychologically safe, or that it can safely intrude upon interpersonal relationships without hopelessly confusing and undermining them. And even if the "experiment" goes badly, it goes on.

To such questions a Christian brings an understanding of person and relationship that is based ultimately in the pattern of the Trinity, in which the three divine identities share the perfect mutuality of the divine community that is the Trinity. Within that common life, each person of the Trinity relates to the others, and in these relationships each is said to be a person. In much the same way, human personhood arises from relationships of mutuality in community. Will cloning, will germ line modification, so distort the mutuality of relationship that it reduces the modified child to an artifact, an engineering project, an achievement to be shown off? Or is it possible to use these technologies within the mutuality of relationship? I do not know, and I do not think anyone knows. But I am sure we ought to ponder this before we act.

Actions that affect relationships also affect social structures, the third of our themes and one that is usually neglected. It should be obvious that if such things as germ line modification will actually bring the benefits its advocates promise, these benefits are likely to be distributed unevenly. More worrisome is that these benefits—better health, perhaps someday the enhancement of mental or other abilities—are exactly the sorts of assets that will widen the gap between those who can afford them and those who cannot. Today's wealth will buy not mere toys or luxuries but advantages for creating future wealth and privilege. How this will affect an already stratified society or affect relationships between nations can only be imagined.

When we think about the question of social justice as it relates
to a new technology, we have to ask first whether the technology is
a good that must be fairly distributed or an evil from which all must
be fairly protected. Indeed, in some religious statements, we sometimes learn that genetic engineering is a great evil *and* that the poor
must get their fair share of it. Fairness of distribution, of itself, cannot determine the value of what is distributed. In the case of
biotechnology, there are both benefits and risks, and we must insist
on some level of equity in the distribution of both. It would be doubly unfair to test an AIDS vaccine in Africa, exposing people there
to the risk, only to price a successful vaccine above their means.

The earliest applications of such technologies as germ line
modification will likely not go to the rich but to the medically
needy, who by virtue of that circumstance can be as vulnerable as
the poor and might consent to the risk of experimentation out of
sheer desperation. Informed consent alone is not a sufficient protection, even if we were to figure out how to extend its meaning to
include unborn generations. But once germ line modification is
past the experimental stage, after a period of twenty to fifty years,
and once it becomes feasible to achieve some real benefit, then we
can be sure that the wealthy who can buy these benefits will want
to do so. Some of these benefits might be deliverable at low cost
and therefore widely distributed, but it is almost certain that there
will always be an upper end of high-cost, high-benefit strategies.
One could argue that even so, *all* are better off under such an
arrangement, but not if it contributes to the further widening of
gaps. Quite likely, the benefits of technology will be far less potent
than we expect them to be, but in a sense this only makes matters
worse, at least as depicted in the film *Gattaca*. The enhanced are
not really better performers than the unenhanced, and yet because
they are thought to be so, positions of power are reserved for them.

Lee Silver imagines that in time, the social gap between the
enhanced and the unenhanced will be so wide that it becomes a
biological gap, and human beings will separate into two species.
This seems highly unlikely, but it does bring us again to the question of human destiny, our fourth and final theme. Consider for a
moment where our species has come from and where we are going.
We have emerged through natural processes, and in us nature has

attained awareness of itself, and with awareness, a sense of awe, obligation, and gratitude. *And* a right to meddle? A right to rewrite the genes that bear the legacy of our evolution, a right to remake ourselves? For some, such as the great philosopher of technology Hans Jonas, this is the essence of folly:

> Now, this innate sufficiency of human nature, which we must posit as the enabling premise for any creative steering of destiny, and which is nothing other than the sufficiency (albeit fallible) for truth, valuation, and freedom, is a thing unique and stupendous to behold in the stream of becoming, out of which it emerged, which in essence it transcends, but by it can also be swallowed again . . . Most evidently, the authority which it imparts can never include the disfiguring, endangering, or refashioning of itself. No gain is worth this price, no hope of gain justifies this risk.[6]

In this view, we owe it not merely to ourselves but to *nature as a whole*, to the cosmos, not to act with an irresponsibility that would jeopardize nature's achievement (namely, us human beings) by presuming to replace ourselves with our artifacts.

The question of human destiny, for Christians, is really the question of God's future for the creation. Are we the apex, the best evolution can do, the highest possible achievement of nature? Or is it possible that through us and our technology, nature will transcend itself again, much as when it produced its first "miracles," such as life and consciousness? Will nature transcend itself again via technology and give us—or, as we should say, give God—a transhuman species more intelligent, more spiritual, more loving, more creative, poetic, musical, more adept at praise, more generous, more able to glorify and enjoy God? Could our technology be the midwife of divine creativity, God's hands in our clay?

But even as I ask this question I am aware of its audacity, even its insanity. It is a suggestion that we must reject, if we mean to think of it as a possible human achievement, as if we could create what is truly better than ourselves. We may be able to engineer a few improvements, but we are most likely to eliminate our superficial

---

6. Hans Jonas, *The Imperative of Responsibility: In Search of an Ethics for the Technological Age* (Chicago: University of Chicago Press, 1984), 33.

flaws while enhancing our deepest ones, and so I cannot imagine that we human beings could make a better being. And yet I cannot wholly dismiss the thought that God can use all that lies within the creation to create anew and to go beyond us. God is the creator, and we and our technology are mere creatures, mere instruments, whether we recognize it or not. It is best by far to recognize this and to consent, to offer technology in service and humble praise. But even our refusal does not negate the right of what is greater to use us to make something new, much as viruses and enzymes were used to make us. God orders us and our technology, and so I have to come back to the question and seriously entertain the possibility that our technology can and should be seen as instruments in the creator's hands, by which God will continue to sculpt Adam's clay, refashioning life in the universe so that it might give greater glory to its maker.

Contributors

ERIC BERESFORD is Consultant for Ethics and Interfaith Relations for the Anglican Church of Canada and Consultant for Ethics for the Anglican Communion Office. Previously, he was Assistant Professor for Ethics in the Faculty of Religious Studies at McGill University. He is a priest of the Anglican Church of Canada.

DONALD M. BRUCE is Director of the Society, Religion and Technology Project of the Church of Scotland, working at the interface of technology, theology and society. He is co-author of *Engineering Genesis* on ethics in non-human genetic engineering and a leading authority on the ethics of cloning.

LISA SOWLE CAHILL is J. Donald Monan, SJ, Professor of Theology at Boston College. The author of *Love Your Enemies: Discipleship, Pacifism and Just War Theory, Family: A Christian Social Perspective*, and *Sex and Gender Ethics*, Cahill is a fellow of the American Academy of Arts and Sciences. She has served on the National Conference of Catholic Bishops Marriage and Family Life Committee.

AUDREY R. CHAPMAN is the Director of the Program of Dialogue on Science, Ethics, and Religion at the American Association for the Advancement of Science and an ordained minister of the United Church of Christ. She is the author of *Unprecedented Choices: Religious Ethics at the Frontiers of Genetic Science*, coauthor of *Human Inheritable Genetic Modifications: Assessing Scientific,*

Ethical, Religious, and Policy Issues, and editor of *Perspectives on Genetic Patenting: Religion, Science, and Industry in Dialogue.*

RONALD COLE-TURNER is the H. Parker Sharp Professor of Theology and Ethics at Pittsburgh Theological seminary, author of *The New Genesis* and co-author of *Pastoral Genetics,* editor of *Human Cloning: Religious Responses,* and an ordained minister of the United Church of Christ.

KENNETH W. CULVER received his doctorate in medicine from the University of Iowa and completed his Pediatric and Immunology training at the University of California, San Francisco before moving to the National Institutes of Health in Bethesda, Maryland. Currently he is Executive Director of Pharmacogenetics at Novartis Pharmaceuticals Corporation. He is member of the National Presbyterian Church in Washington D.C.

DEMETRI DEMOPULOS, Ph.D. (genetics), is a parish priest in the Greek Orthodox Church and teaches a course in science and religion at Holy Cross Greek Orthodox School of Theology. He has co-authored articles on maize and human genetics and has lectured nationally and internationally on bioethics and cloning.

NANCY J. DUFF, an ordained Presbyterian minister and Associate Professor of Theological Ethics at Princeton Seminary, wrote *Humanization and the Politics of God: The Koinonia Ethics of Paul Lehmann.* She addressed the National Bioethics Advisory Committee on human cloning and human stem cell research.

GILBERT MEILAENDER holds the Phyllis and Richard Duesenberg Chair in Christian Ethics at Valparaiso University. He is the author of *Body, Soul and Bioethics* and *Bioethics: A Primer for Christians.*

SONDRA WHEELER is the Martha Ashby Carr Professor of Christian Ethics at Wesley Theological Seminary in Washington, D.C. She is the author of *Stewards of Life: Bioethics and Pastoral Care,* as well as numerous articles concerning the intersection of bioethics and Christian theology.